SUPER SKETCHES

FOR YOUTH MINISTRY

ZONDERVAN/YOUTH SPECIALTIES BOOKS

Adventure Games
Amazing Tension Getters
Attention Grabbers for 4th-6th Graders (Get 'Em Growing)
Called to Care
The Complete Student Missions Handbook
Creative Socials and Special Events
Divorce Recovery for Teenagers
Feeding Your Forgotten Soul (Spiritual Growth for Youth Workers)
Get 'Em Talking
Good Clean Fun
Good Clean Fun, Volume 2
Great Games for 4th-6th Graders (Get 'Em Growing)
Great Ideas for Small Youth Groups
Greatest Skits on Earth
Greatest Skits on Earth, Volume 2
Growing Up in America
High School Ministry
High School TalkSheets
Holiday Ideas for Youth Groups (Revised Edition)
Hot Talks
Ideas for Social Action
Intensive Care: Helping Teenagers in Crisis
Junior High Ministry
Junior High TalkSheets
The Ministry of Nurture
On-Site: 40 On-Location Programs for Youth Groups
Option Plays
Organizing Your Youth Ministry
Play It! Great Games for Groups
Quick and Easy Activities for 4th-6th Graders (Get 'Em Growing)
Super Sketches for Youth Ministry
Teaching the Bible Creatively
Teaching the Truth About Sex
Tension Getters
Tension Getters II
Unsung Heroes: How to Recruit and Train Volunteer Youth Workers
Up Close and Personal: How to Build Community in Your Youth Group
Youth Ministry Nuts and Bolts
The Youth Specialties Handbook for Great Camps and Retreats
Youth Specialties Clip Art Book
Youth Specialties Clip Art Book, Volume 2

SUPER SKETCHES
FOR YOUTH MINISTRY

Thirty Creative Topical Dramas
from Willow Creek Community Church

Debra Poling &
Sharon Sherbondy

ZondervanPublishingHouse
Grand Rapids, Michigan

A Division of HarperCollins*Publishers*

Super Sketches for Youth Ministry

Copyright © 1991 by Youth Specialties, Inc.

Youth Specialties Books, 1224 Greenfield Drive, El Cajon, California 92021,
are published by Zondervan Publishing House, Grand Rapids, Michigan 49530

Library of Congress Cataloging-in-Publication Data

Poling, Debra, 1956-
Super Sketches for youth ministry: thirty creative topical dramas for kids from Willow
Creek Community Church / Debra Poling, Sharon Sherbondy
    p.   cm.
ISBN 0-310-53411-9
1. Church work with teenagers. 2. Drama in Christian education. 3. Teenagers—Religious life—Drama. 4. Teenagers—Conduct of life—Drama. I. Sherbondy, Sharon,
1953-. II. Willow Creek Community Church (South Barrington, Ill.) III. Title.
BV4447.P57 1991
246.7—dc20   90-49193
                                                CIP

Edited by J. Cheri McLaughlin
Design and Typography by Jamison · Bell Advertising and Design

Printed in the United States of America

      94 95 96 97 98 99 / CH / 10 9 8 7 6 5 4

To our husbands, Judson and Steve,
for your vision, support, and unending encouragement

Deb and Sharon

TABLE OF CONTENTS

FOREWORD

The authors of this book have marked my life multiple times through their drama ministries. They have made me laugh and cry, they have made me see myself for who I am, and they have helped me see God for who He is! I celebrate the giftedness of these two women and count it a great privilege to co-labor with them at Willow Creek Community Church and around the world.

Bill Hybels
Pastor
Willow Creek Community Church

PREFACE

For the past 15 years I've labored to help students understand spiritual truth—the life changing truth the Bible teaches. Anyone who has attempted this task knows the extreme challenge it represents.

Along the road I've discovered the amazing effectiveness of well done drama presentations in stirring students to think and feel. Kids are visually oriented—I think we all know that. The question is, "How do we capitalize on this reality of the student culture?" Well, I know two people who can help you in a very tangible way. Sharon S. and Deb P. have both effectively, within the context of real student ministry, demonstrated their ability to write and direct dramatic presentations and sketches that connect with students. This book can help you do the same. I encourage you to read it carefully.

Dan Webster
Director of Student Ministries
Willow Creek Community Church

*S*ince this is a book for Christian leaders, we really *should* start with a Bible reference, right? Do you remember 1 Corinthians 9:22, where it says

to "be all things to all *kids*" (paraphrase ours)? Well, just as Paul mingled with the pagans and adapted his preaching to their culture, so must we. Students live their lives in a world unfamiliar to us. Acclimating ourselves to their milieu is prerequisite to trying to reshape it – and kids know whether we truly understand them or not. Can we blame them if they reject our message about *unseen* realities when we apparently don't comprehend what they *do* see every day?

Our teens are living in a society of fast-moving sights, wild sounds, high-tech toys, and low-tech values. To make contact

with them, we need to broadcast on a familiar wavelength. Since computerized laser-light shows and Dolby-recorded 70mm movies are beyond the budget of most youth groups, we offer *Super Sketches for Youth Ministry.* Live drama gives you a chance to speak teens' language, showing them you know (and care) about them and their world. (It's also a lot cheaper than renting Vari-Lites and fog machines.)

Dramatic sketches not only show kids we understand their world, they also let kids see that God wants to be involved in their lives. We've probably become callous to how shocked (in a positive way) high-school students

are to discover that God actually wants to relate to them personally, on their home field. Jesus met Saul on the road to Damascus. (Jesus had last been seen outside Jerusalem – who traveled to whom?)

Student Impact, the high-school ministry of Willow Creek Community Church, stresses (among other things) the importance of knowing our audience. Who is it we're trying to reach? Our students speak English, so we don't give powerful, Scripture-based, Holy Spirit-anointed messages in French. Yet so often the approach taken in youth ministry sounds foreign to teens. A serious task of any cross-cultural missionary is to learn the language and customs of the targeted people. Anyone in youth work needs to acquire such information and skills to penetrate the youth subculture. Effective communicators work hard to keep up with what is current with teens – what's the latest thing turning their cranks? As Student Impact staff, whether we agree with what is being presented or not, we go to see the latest movies, we study popular sitcoms, we're informed about who are the hottest music groups, and we even try to stay aware of popular drugs.

Super Sketches puts dating, family, self-esteem, peer pressure, abortion, alcoholism, child abuse, suicide, and more right in front of their faces – live – screaming to them, "We *know* what you are faced with! We know how awful it is. Yes, sometimes we can laugh, even in pain, but that's only because we've truly embraced how dark it feels." Being able to relate to students with this kind of penetrating empathy builds a credibility that invites them to stay for more.

These sketches, while not giving answers, are perfect set ups for messages. Imagine speaking to a youth group when they've seen and identified with a sketch about suicide. Think of the greater impact you'll have when you talk about sins of the tongue and the audience has already laughed at themselves as they've watched a drama about gossip. Drama is a window of honesty and integrity that can frame *their* world – and show them you have something of value to say to them. "Pre-preach" connections like this are possible through drama, and this book can help you get started.

These sketches are also designed as springboards for further interaction. Discussion questions that further emphasize biblical principles follow each sketch. The emotions that these sketches trigger create passageways for support and encouragement to enter deep into the hearts of kids.

We are convinced of God's care and

grace to meet us where ever we are, whatever language we speak, whatever form of communication we relate to. God's love extends far beyond any mess we could possibly get into and we are committed to do whatever we can so that our teens will be able to embrace his love. We've found that getting dramatic about it helps make our point. Now, with this book, you can too.

—Deb Poling and
Sharon Sherbondy

PART ONE

How to Use This Book

As I think back on the most significant memories of working with drama teams, it's not been the impact of the medium that stands out (although that is far more significant than I often realize). What I remember are the kids – how green and starry-eyed they were the first few weeks of meeting together. I remember the battles – I had to be firm with accountability. I recall how embarrassed yet pleased I felt when they started riding me for not doing what I expected them to do.

"I remember one of the strongest, biggest, jock-type guys crying after he was made to look stupid because someone else forgot their lines. I remember trying to silence another team member who kept forget-ting he wasn't the director – all the while hoping I wasn't hinder-ing his creativity. I remember taking the team to perform for another youth group and feeling tender and proud when, at the conclusion of the performance, they went out into the group to talk with the other kids.

"Through hard confrontations, sharing a common goal, and try-ing not to gloss over even the most minute relational problems, we developed a chemistry that allowed team members to be free to perform and minister through drama."

—Deb Poling

CHAPTER ONE

Sounds Like a Lot of Work—For What?

(or Why Use Drama?)

Right now, someone in your youth group is reading, "Have *safe* sex" (translate – sex outside marriage is okay). Another student just saw an ad on MTV: "Designate a driver" (translate – take turns getting drunk). Think of the voices calling out to kids, the images invading their eyes and minds, daily commending some of the following ideas:

The perfect body is attainable.
Fun is synonymous with partying.
Self-esteem is tied directly to wearing the right clothes.
Wealth and possessions lead to the good life.
Love is a feeling and has nothing to do with commitment.
Violence is acceptable if someone really deserves it.

Then here we come, believers, messengers of a new way to live, talk, talk, talk, talk, talking the ancient words of a distant God. We say, "God's way is the best." They say, "Oh, yeah? Show me."

How do we reach these video-saturated souls with a message

written on gilded, leather-bound pages, when the last piece of leather they saw was the pants of their favorite rock star? Everything that's shaped their values they've *seen* somewhere: life at home, life with their peer group, TV programs, movies. Even their music, the last bastion of a nonvisual mode of communication, has been brought into the two-dimensional world of the cathode-ray tube via music videos – they now watch their music, too.

What's a Youth Worker to Do?

Lamenting the loss of our children's literacy provides hours of engaging discussion, but meanwhile, a generation goes to hell without any competing alternative images. Wouldn't it be better to reach kids by presenting our message in the images and voices they confront daily? Ways exist to show kids we know their struggles, not only by speaking to *them*, but by allowing them to see their *peers* enmeshed in the same battles. We can *show* kids we understand their humor, their feelings, their thoughts. They can see and feel that God's message is for them. Christian drama can be an excellent, accessible medium to complement our youth programs and combat the deteriorating effects of our culture.

Kids do want guidance, they want answers, and they definitely want to know they are loved. Behind their barbed exteriors, they are still children – children faced with challenges that would crumple most adults. They need to know someone cares enough to enter into their lives and lead them. But they won't just open up to anybody. They shouldn't.

Through drama, as they see the issues they confront acted out, they may become more receptive to hearing what God has to say. Once they feel understood they're more likely to say, "Tell me more," and willingly enter into discussions on a heart-to-heart level. They may allow a new opening in their walls – they may even do away with some of the walls that keep them from experiencing the Christian life.

People often ask, "Why drama? What's the big deal about it, anyway?" We love this question because the biblical precedent is so much fun to talk about – Jesus was given to theatrics. Think of the stories he told. Notice how they relate to the culture of his day: a man taking his inheritance and ending up longing to eat pig's food; the benefits of construction on a solid foundation versus sand; comparing humans to fish, trees ... even dirt! Think about the dramatic ways Jesus chose to make a point: walking on water, stretching dinner to satisfy five thousand, spitting on the ground and using the resulting mud to heal a man's eyes. Come on, give us a break! Spit-made mud?!

What about God the Father – the ultimate creative genius? Who else could have thought up a scenario as unbelievable as this: Jonah is running in the wrong direction, and God sucks him up into a fish. Talk about forced solitude for prayer and meditation! The writers of soap operas can't come close to God's writing of Joseph's life: favoritism by daddy, severe sibling rivalry, living life in the pits (literally), being a slave-turned-ruler, falsely charged with adultery, having the opportunity to take revenge on slimy brothers.

How about these examples of reinforcing principles with pictures: Long for the old life? Poof! You're a pillar of salt. Try to pass a little white lie about how much you put in the offering? Tsk, tsk! You'll never lie again – or eat, or think, or breathe. Try to fight against God's army? He gets his jazz band playing, and crash, your walls dance all the way to the ground.

Why all these remarkable audio-visuals? Is God giving instructions on what to do if we ever find ourselves thrown into a pit by our brothers, or to instruct us that when fleeing a burning city we shouldn't look back? No! God gave us these wild memories so that we can connect with the struggles people have always had, even if the circum-stances aren't as unusual. And he did it *dramatically*.

He wants us to know that he understands the feeling of wanting to run from him. He wants us to be able to say, "Wow, I can relate to feeling ripped off by my family, just like Joseph."

Dramatic sketches attempt to show little capsules of life today for the purpose of getting I-can-relate-to-that-feeling responses. When that happens, we've made a connection. We've become credible to the kids.

Then Drama's All I Need?

Although identification with kids and their culture prefaces effective ministry to kids, and although drama can be a powerful tool to build that credibility, there are some things that drama *doesn't* do well. If you're looking for God in every sketch, you'll have to read between the lines. Christian drama doesn't always say "God." It *does* present biblical principles: the destructive effects of sin, the meaninglessness of life without Christ, the difficulty of growing up without the right guidance. It raises

> Christian drama doesn't always say "God." It does present biblical principles.

questions relating to values, often showing the emptiness of our culture's standards. But it usually stops short of supplying a three-point-outline alternative.

Gimmicks fail to penetrate kids. A successful program consists of more than just good music or entertaining dramas – drama isn't meant to do everything. It's strength is in breaking down barriers. By means of drama we connect with kids within the culture they know, building relationships that demonstrate our care and offer help. An effective dramatic sketch shows kids a bit of sanity in life's confusion, without oversimplifying that confusion. By avoiding three-point how-to's, we respect their process without abandoning them in their turmoil. Kids whose parents are going through a divorce need a friend, someone to care. They *will* eventually get over the pain, but pointing to future relief without standing with them for a while in their grief and anger doesn't fulfill the biblical injunction to "weep with those who weep." Job's friends sat with him in silence for several days. Then they messed up – they started "comforting" him by talking.

When building relationships with hurting kids, and even more so when we're putting together messages, we're often tempted to answer the unspoken question, "Why?" What kids really need to know is, "What now?" The emotional walls built by teens are protective: they keep pain out, they keep some semblance of self-worth locked in. Yet those walls are not set, yet. And there are some openings. Although kids may close their front door of direct verbal contact to parents and teachers, drama lets us come in the back door.

So What's the Catch?

Kids have developed a taste for CD's, TV shows, and blockbuster movies produced by million-dollar budgets and big-name artists. We know we can't directly compete with high-tech, high-cost entertainment. Yet we can strive for excellence with what we have. Kids will scrutinize the content, judge the integrity, assess the quality, and critique the presentation of dramatic sketches (as they will every other aspect of our ministry). This means more work for you, and your team. There, we said it. The biggest thing standing in the way of effectively using drama in youth ministry is not lack of talent or giftedness, but *lack of effort*. Dependance on God fills in our deficiencies with Holy Spirit-instilled creativity and insight – so don't cut yourself short. Give the Holy Spirit some planning and rehearsal time to work with. These sketches don't require expensive sets, elaborate costumes, or professional stages. They will come to life by putting energy into them – and by maintaining a constant commitment to excellence.

But a drama ministry impacts more than its audience. Preparing and presenting effective dramatic sketches can also be of enormous value to the students on the drama team. Kids with creative communication gifts receive training, their leaders gain expertise, and the drama team provides a support system for its members – a healthy peer group to connect with. Kids have to belong. They will sacrifice their self-esteem, values, health, Levi jeans, even their virginity to feel they belong. If done right, the drama team can give them a sense of belonging, a sense that they matter, without having to compromise their beliefs. Who knows? They may even grow up a bit.

Drama is work for the youth leader as well as the kids, make no mistake. If it's not challenging from time to time, then you're doing something wrong. Webster defines a leader as "a horse placed in advance of the other horses of a team." Okay, so that's not the primary definition. But we thought it fit. If a lead horse (that is, *you*) harnesses up with the team, and then says, "All right, guys, you take this cart to the finish line. I'll just stick my face in this feed bag till we get there," who would go? They'd all want to feed their faces, too. But if you invest in the kids, care for them, and navigate the turns in front of them, they will use their strength to promote the ministry.

And the rewards of the race (blue ribbons and flower-covered horseshoes) outweigh the effort. (All right, maybe not always on this side of heaven.) This ministry is worth it for the adult leaders. This ministry is worth it for the team. This ministry is worth it for the students you're trying to reach.

Drama ministry is worth it!

How Do I Get This Thing Off the Ground?

Us: You've continued on to Chapter Two. That's a good sign.

You: I may as well – I paid for the book. But even if I *do* want to do this drama thing, I don't know any more about directing than I do about dirigibles!

Us: Let us explain – a dirigible is an air-bag, a director is an air-head …

Now you're going to learn everything about acting and directing and rehearsals and performances in one easy chapter. (If you believe that, you really are an air-head!)

First, we need to get something off our chests. This is a book of sketches, not skits. "What's the difference?" you ask. Simply this: **Skits** serve the purpose of allowing anyone in your youth group to let loose, have fun, get attention, and make others laugh. **Sketches**, on the other hand, are for communicating life truths. All those other fun things may happen, but with a sketch, the point is to make a point. Sound confusing? Following is a

chart to help explain the differences.

Skits have their place, but they do not mix well with sketches. Don't plan a skit night, then throw in a sketch in an attempt to add substance to the evening. As you have seen, skits and sketches serve very different purposes. Please, don't treat the sketches in this book as you would skits. We wrote purposefully, attempting to meet some specific needs of teenagers. These sketches, even the humorous ones, work only if they are handled with the same integrity with which they were written.

There, the point has been made. We feel better now. Thank you.

* * * * *

Skit	*Sketch*
1. Usually improvisational—created quickly and often not written down.	1. Follows the pattern of formal play writing, including rising action (a beginning), which leads to a main conflict (a middle), and then moves to some form of resolution (an ending). And the ending often does not resolve the conflict. In fact, in the sketches that follow, you'll discover we rarely tie everything up in neat packages. Life's problems are not always followed by tidy answers.
2. Usually humorous (or tries to be).	
3. Used as an outlet for goofing around and having fun.	
4. Audience watches and enjoys but stays detached from action.	2. Encompasses all emotions—fear, joy, anger, sadness, affection, etc. Of course, not all in one sketch.
5. Not done to stimulate life changes in the audience. *Example*: A short-man skit employing the gimmick of one person hiding behind another and using his hands as feet to give the illusion of a very short person. It doesn't matter much what is communicated. It's just for fun.	3. Designed to draw attention to a character, not the actor. Sketches don't work if the actors don't try to lose themselves in their roles.
	4. To be taken seriously. Has integrity and substance. Presented artistically.
	5. Audience participates by being drawn in emotionally. The audience sees some of themselves, connects personally to the conflict, and is "moved." A sketch has the potential to change lives. *Example*: The sketches in this book.

Us: Now let's get into the specifics of how to form a drama team.

You: It's about time!

Us: First we have to tell you about directors.

You: You mean (gulp), you're going to talk about more work for *me*?

Us: Aw, come on. You'll like this part.

We've emphasized the importance of excellence, and the significance of devoting time to this endeavor. Yet we are not insane enough to assume that you have decades of free time to pour into a drama team. So how can it be done? For you, easily, really: *get someone else to do it!* (And you thought we were totally insensitive!)

The director of Student Impact has never been, and never will be, the director of the drama team. The drama director has typically been an adult (loosely defined as anyone over twenty) who has an interest in drama. (Notice we said *adult*. We would not recommend using students to direct their peers. The potential problems are obvious.) We have at times paid our directors and at other times had volunteer directors.

Past directors of the Student Impact drama team have all had a passion for drama ministry, though we've not all had prior callings to work with teenagers. The two of us, for example, were both members of Willow Creek's adult drama team when we were asked to direct the youths. In almost every church, there must be at least one person who would love to head up the youth drama ministry – the youth leader shouldn't do it all. It's no good having a drama team that is led by a "fried" youth pastor. Allow others to use their gifts to oversee the team. If you can't immediately find a director with whom you feel comfortable, at least recruit an assistant to be a gofer. That person may eventually gain enough confidence to take over the team.

One caution: Directors need to maintain a close working relationship with youth pastors. They cannot go off and do their own thing – we are very comfortable knowing we are under the ultimate direction of the youth pastor. We see the drama team as enhancing the direction of the entire youth group, and we encourage any other would-be directors to stay humble about their role in the ministry. For some reason people with artistic tendencies – us included – often resist working as a team. We have found, however, that

> **Directors cannot go off and do their own thing— we see the drama team as enhancing the direction of the entire youth group.**

when we let go of our need to have things go our way and allow others to improve our work through thoughtful criticism, everyone benefits in the long run. Whether you're the drama director or the youth pastor, don't let the drama team become isolated from the rest of the youth ministry.

So now you can see that when we refer to *director*, it means drama director, whoever that may be.

Goofy Kids Can't Always Act

As the drama director, you take on the role of talent scout. Fully engage your radar as you seek out students who display an ability to communicate honestly. Don't be deceived by the goofy kids; they like to have the attention drawn to themselves and therefore are often not good at sketches. Remember the comparison between skits and sketches? A sketch requires actors who can lose themselves in their characters. You're building a ministry team, so you must do what Jesus did – pick and choose. We suggest you personally invite potential actors to audition as well as announce to the entire group the time for auditioning. Any others besides your handpicked hopefuls who come and surprise you with their talents are "whipped cream." Occasionally, good actors are the loners who hide in the woodwork.

* * * * *

You: You're serious – you expect me to have auditions! Don't you realize I'm going to have a mutiny if I refuse anyone?

Us: Perhaps, but you'll survive. And we've got some ideas for involving all the other interested kids. Besides, trials produce endurance, right?

You: Shut up.

Being the director gives you a distinct advantage over those auditioning. They *fear* you. They're *terrified* of what you are going to make them do. They're *petrified* of making fools of themselves. So relax about auditions – you've got it made. It may be the only time you'll have that much power.

Announce the date, place, and time for the auditions and get sign-ups. Make sure the students you have pursued also sign up. Don't give anyone the special favor of not needing to audition. You'll have egomaniacal monsters on your hands. Fairness is crucial both for the students' benefit and your integrity as the director.

One of two things will probably happen when you announce auditions: everyone will sign up and you'll be able to pick the cream of the crop, or no one will sign up and you'll have to offer them cash. Actually, in the latter event, because you sought out some kids personally, you're covered without the bribes. What if you have only one or two kids to work with? Then you can skip auditions. Work with those you have – two-person sketches can be very powerful. Don't expect to perform dramas weekly. In time the periodic presentation of sketches will generate more interest, and other kids will want to get involved. Or generate interest just before auditions by selecting a few kids to do a one-time performance for the whole group of one of the sketches, such as "To Leap or Not to Leap" or "A Dime a Dozen." Allow yourself plenty of time to rehearse so that the presentation is a positive experience rather than a disaster no one wants to repeat.

Audition Day: What Do I Do?

The most important impression you can give to the kids on audition day is that of being organized.

Arrive early. Have everything you need laid out and ready to use by the time anyone else arrives. Have enough copies of scripts on hand – no last minute runs to the copier. Take charge, but of course, also be fun and relaxed. Being well prepared sends a powerful, non-verbal message of the expectations you have for drama team members. Make drama a high calling instead of something students can take or leave.

Request personal summaries. The first thing we do when we audition kids for Student Impact's drama team is to have them each fill out a personal summary form. Often we give this form to the kids when they sign up for auditions, asking them to bring it to auditions completed. Students who do not receive the form in advance are given time to fill it out during auditions. We don't let anyone leave without giving us a completed form.

On the personal summary form we ask for the student's name, address, phone number, age, employment, and work phone number. Then we get more personal. We ask:

How long have you attended Student Impact?
Are you involved in any other area of service?
Tell us about your Christian experience (that is, your testimony).
What training and/or experience do you have in drama?
Describe briefly why you want to get involved with the drama team.

Don't read the summaries right then – you'll need all the time you can get for the other aspects of the auditions.

Explain expectations. We tell the kids up front our expectations for drama team members. Here are ours, to get you thinking about what you might include:

1) Participants must have a personal commitment to Christ and want to use their talents to benefit others.

COMMENTS: We have been asked, "What if the aspiring actor is not a believer, or is a borderline believer?" We wish we could quote a verse that spelled out specifically what to do, such as, "If a teen wants to get involved in the performing arts for ministry purposes and is not yet a follower of Jesus, he must first purify himself by washing his clothing in Tide seven times seventy and memorize the ingredients in his shampoo."

We can see the benefit of using the arts to bring students into a place where they can hear the gospel. The drama team, however, is a visible group, and therefore those in it are perceived as representatives of Christ alive in the here and now. Non-Christians (or marginal believers) won't demonstrate the lifestyle you're telling kids God offers (or wants). We must ask, "How can a person minister to others when that person is unaware of who or what the ministry is for?" Don't get caught putting a talented but spiritually aloof teen on stage out of desperation. It confuses students to see someone who doesn't stand for God *pretending to* in front of a crowd. Ability alone, unsurrendered to the leadership of Jesus Christ, cannot bear lasting fruit. The experience damages the teen who pretends and misleads the students who are trying to see if Christians really are different from the rest of the world.

Having given that warning, we grant that, providing their lifestyles are not an embarrassment to Christ, immature believers with soft hearts toward God *might* be helped to full commitment to Christ through joining the team. Caution: Don't put borderline believers in the limelight too early. Give them time to be involved in the team with smaller parts before assigning any central roles. Explain openly to them why you are holding back.

2) Commitment to drama team involves one full school year. This includes attending regularly scheduled meetings, rehearsals, and performances, and coming to rehearsals with *lines memorized*; not being late, tardy, slow in arriving, waiting to arrive until things get going, or arriving on time to the rest rooms and not the rehearsal room or anything like that.

COMMENTS: I guess we have this thing for timeliness! Actually, as those who've worked in the arts can attest, there can be no excellence without discipline. Punctuality is the easiest measurement of discipline (or lack of it) and can be a place where commitment is tested on a practical level. Demanding punctuality tells the kids that you expect them to reach high standards.

3) **If you are unable to make a rehearsal, contact the director in advance. Only two unexcused absences are allowed (in other words, if you don't show up and have not bothered to give us your excuse in advance, you earn an unexcused absence). Three strikes and you're out! And we mean it.**

COMMENTS: Unity and trust are built through commitment to one another. Maybe we're crazy for expecting so much, but this is what our drama team needed. Of course, these are suggestions, not gospel truth. If you require less from your team, however, you may experience a breakdown in commitment that will undermine the effectiveness of the drama team's ministry.

4) **Every member must be willing to help out with all aspects of the drama ministry: getting props, making costumes and sets, prompting, encouraging those who are acting, etc.**

COMMENTS: A team is a team.

5) **To get the best parts in the sketch, pay off the director. (Just kidding!)**

Audition Warm-Ups

It's now time to get the auditions underway. Rather than handing out a preaudition assignment or holding a talent show, we use theater games and script reading to evaluate what the kids can do. Before script readings we loosen up and relax the group as much as possible. Remember how the nerd in *Sixteen Candles* acted when he was getting ready to ask Molly Ringwald to dance? He was standing in the back of the gym with his weird friends, and he began jumping around and wiggling his shoulders and rotating his head and breathing deeply and slapping his face to get every part of his body alive. Have the group get in a large circle and do that same thing. Let them laugh and feel foolish. You do it with them and feel foolish, too.

Then lead them in some stretching

> Unity and trust are built through commitment to one another. This is what our drama team needed.

and bending exercises – like warming up for a race – to warm up their bodies to act. To warm up their voices, ask the group to recite "Mary Had a Little Lamb" in unison. Direct them to say it softly, then scream it, then say it with sadness, then with happiness, fear, anger, etc.

Now move into some improvisational theater games – Who, What, Where, for instance, is easy and fun to use. In one box place slips of paper on which you write descriptions of characters – the *Who* of the improvisation (for example, eighty-five-year-old cowboy, ten-year-old spoiled brat, sixteen-year-old ultra-jock, Aunt Mabel, drug addict, nerd). Let your imagination go. In a second box place descriptions of locations – the *Where* of the improvisation (for example, cow judging at a state fair, a Hawaiian luau, an ocean liner stuck in a storm, a waiting room in a veterinarian's office).

Divide the kids into groups of two to four. Each young person picks one slip of paper from the *Who* box, and each group picks one slip of paper from the *Where* box. Once each group has selected their *Who* and *Where* slips, give them a few minutes to decide the problem, disagreement, or main event on which the improv will focus – the *What*. They aren't to sketch out a play-by-play description of what will happen, but rather they should select a particular event for the characters to interact within (for example, something is stolen, you ran over my dog, you threw up on me, etc.).

Give the groups five minutes to discuss how they plan to use their characters, location, and event to create a performance for the rest of the people at the audition. When a group is ready to start, one of its members says, "curtain." Set a time limit for each improv, two to three minutes at most. Give the actors a thirty-second warning that time is running out so they can wrap it up somehow. As you are enjoying this improvisation, remember that your goal is to determine which kids are able to lead and stay in character. This game can reveal those with potential.

Audition Readings

Effective actors do more than simply express emotion, project, and lose themselves in their characters; they also work well with other actors, have a feel for timing and movement, and are aware of what's going on around them. The scripts you choose for audition readings should give as much variety as possible, and you should only do a portion of each script. This is where preparation is essential. You will need to bring two types of scripts: monologues (like "Loneliness") to showcase the actor's ability to emote, and a multi-character sketch ("My Lips Are Sealed" and "Caterpillar Flight" work well) for observing teamwork. Select a sketch that includes some humor to get an idea of how the actors handle comedy. Have enough copies of all the scripts so that the kids have something to work on while others are auditioning. Tell the kids that you are looking for expressiveness and characterization, as well as the ability to sense timing and work as a team player. Tell them not to try to memorize the lines but to concentrate on being the character, both in sound and movement. Allow them ten minutes to practice, then start calling them in, one group or monologue at a time. Encourage them, tell them to breathe deeply and project. If you have the gift of mercy, give them a second chance.

* * * * *

You: What do I do while these kids are sweating and acting their little thespian hearts out?

Us: You become the almighty judge, the lord of the room, the czar, the "determinator." (Ah, we love getting theatrical!)

Audition Criteria

As the students act, your role is to observe – and you observe with the following three objectives in mind:

How does the actor sound?
Diction: Does he pronounce words clearly?
Volume: Can he be heard? Does he speak dynamically, using the full range of loud and soft?
Expression: Does he sound like the heart monitor of a dead person, or does he have life in his voice?

How does the actor look?
Movement: Does she move? Are her motions natural or contrived? Does she seem to have an awareness of what her hands and feet are doing while her mouth is making sound?
Stage presence: Is she communicating to the audience while staying in character? Is she believable?
Interaction: Does she work well with other actors? Is she aware of and reacting to the others? Is she aware of what the entire scene looks like in relation to where she is?

How does the actor make me feel?
Credibility: Do I sense subjectively that the actor exhibits *realness* in his acting? Do I want to watch this actor? Do I hold my breath until he's finished because he is so pathetic? Do I sense honesty in his emotions? Do I believe his range of emotions? An evaluation of "feel" sounds some-

thing like, "Yeah, he could work well," or else, "I'm not so sure about this kid. Probably not."

You can develop point systems, charts, graphs, and computer programs to help choose the team. Whatever works best for you is fine, as long as you remember **sound**, **look**, and **feel**.

One last significant step in the selection process is a personal interview. After you have read the personal summaries and viewed the auditions, we suggest meeting with each prospective drama team member individually. Take them out for Cokes and use the time to get a better feel of who they are. Are you sure they will be good additions to the team? An informal half hour of interaction is well worth the time in the long run.

As far as frequency of auditions, we do not allow kids to enter the team any time they surface. At most we occasionally hold mid-year auditions. Our reasons: (1) We work hard to build unity within the team. New members entering at random times disrupt that growing trust; (2) Lasting through a waiting period helps confirm a person's commitment to the ministry, as opposed to the glitz.

"Don't Call Us ... We'll Call You."

You've narrowed down the list and are about to tell the group who made the team and who didn't. But before you do any rash cutting of aspiring actors, have you given thought to your need for props, costumes, stage hands, prompters, possibly even lighting and sound engineers? Who is going to take care of all these needs? You? Ha! We spit in your face! As you make your final selections for the drama team, consider putting some of the nonactors to work backstage.

Let the kid with the wonderful talent for drawing make some of the props you will need. Or put the kid who's always making paper airplanes out of the Sunday bulletin to work making coffee-can spotlights. The great thing about a drama ministry is that so many gifts and talents can be used. You may even develop a separate team of stagehands who take great pride in being the backbone of the drama ministry's effectiveness. We did.

* * * * *

You: I've got only three kids wanting to blow my brains out because I didn't include them in the drama group. Not bad, eh?

Us: We usually consider anything under five death threats a success.

You: Now what? I just give them the script and we do it?

Us: Yep. That's it! Have fun.

You: Great. Thanks for the help.

Us: We were just kidding. But you knew that, didn't you?

You: Uh, yeah ... right ... ha, ha, pretty funny.

Us: Before we tell you how to get the sketch ready to perform, we have to talk about taking a group of hyperactive, narcissistic, loud-mouthed, rude, crude renegades and transforming them into a cohesive team.

You: And these students were hand-picked?

The function of any ministry is to build up believers and reach out to un-believers, not just to accomplish program goals. As youth directors and drama directors, our purpose is ultimately "to prepare God's people for works of service, so that the body of Christ may be built up" (Eph. 4:12). Effective ministries flourish because the members grow and develop personal bonds as they do God's work. In other words, they get more out of it than they put in. The drama team is no exception. They need to spend time together – eating, laughing, praying, and performing as a family. Eventually, out of their service to the youth group will flow significant service to each other.

In fact, we might go so far as to say that the ability to trust each other is more important than wonderful acting.

(Ohhh, we can't believe we just wrote that!) You will be asking teenagers to perform possibly embarrassing, memo-rized sketch in front of their peers, totally trusting other actors not to screw up. If they don't know each other well enough to feel they can depend upon each other, you are headed for a disaster.

Because we're both actors, we have had nightmares (the middle-of-the-night ac-tual dream kind) about getting up on stage to perform a sketch and forgetting lines, or get-ting the script two minutes before the per-formance, or making a stage entrance only to realize that others are counting on us and we have no idea what to say. We have also had real-life nightmares of delivering a line to an-other actor who responds with that blank, scared-out-of-his-mind stare that screams, "I don't know what to say next!" – and then going blank our-selves.

> We have had real-life nightmares of delivering a line to another actor who responds with that blank, scared-out-of-his mind stare.

We'll never forget one sketch in which Deb had a short solo rap to mu-sic. "I was full of energy, cruising along through it without a care," she recalls, "until the terminal displaying the lines in my mind had a power failure and the screen went blank. The music continued to race past at record-breaking speed; physically, I kept doing what I was supposed to do, but with no ability to utter a sound. The only thing that squeezed out of my frozen vocal chords was, "C'mon, Baby!" Fortunately, I regained power and spit out the last few lines before retreating to the sanctity of the rest of the performers as we rapped through to the end of the sketch. I knew that I could trust the others to keep going, and that they wouldn't kill me, for blowing it, after the sketch ended."

Acting is a high-anxiety sport. Even after years of performing, the scare remains. "What if *this* is the time I blow it so bad that I die?" Mixing teens, who are at the height of their developmental insecurity, with that kind of pressure leaves even the most confident needing support. One of the best places for receiving that support is within the group.

The Two Golden Rules

To avoid overloading our new drama-team members, we have condensed the many instructions concerning ministry into the framework of two golden rules.

Golden Rule Number One

Real life is where you earn credibility — the message you communicate as an actor on stage will be believable only if you communicate that same message when you live out your offstage roles as friend, son or daughter, and Christian.

We know you know this. We know you tell this to your kids. But they won't hear it the first time — or the second or the third. They need regular reminders that by putting themselves up in front of their peers, they automatically become role models in all areas of their lives — even those areas they think of as private or invisible.

We've been on the "team member" side of things. Sharon was vacationing on a cruise ship on the other side of the country when a stranger came up to her and said, "Aren't you in the drama group from Willow Creek?" We and our food have been stared at in restaurants ("I wonder what the drama group eats?"). We've been recognized going into movies, exercising, shopping. Whether your youth group is made up of fifteen or five hundred teens, the members of the drama team will be watched by them on and off the stage. Their motives for participating in the drama team (whether service or self-promotion, ministry or me-building) will show through in other areas of their lives. And it will reflect on the authenticity of the drama team, your youth program, and possibly your church.

* * * * *

You: Are you telling me that I have to have only perfect little saints or else the drama team is doomed?

Us: Yes. (Just kidding.) If we held out for perfect kids, nothing would ever get done. A good drama team needs kids who know they are not perfect and are honest enough to admit it.

You: Well, great. This sounds so wonderful, so chummy, so deep. I've got kids that have spent so much time imitating peers that they don't even know who they are yet. Got a sledgehammer to break through their walls?

Us: K-Mart sells an excellent one for under twenty-five dollars!

We've discovered a variety of activities, aside from the rehearsals, to help the team open up, get comfortable, and grow in authenticity. First we include fun – take the team to a movie or live theater and then critique it over pizza. Allow them the freedom to express their feelings and thoughts about the show. Plan parties for the team only. Organize a one- or two-day retreat and fill the time with craziness

and closeness. Put kids in the hot seat and let others ask them personal questions. Provide opportunities for actors to talk about their faith with others on the team. Pray together. Have brief devotions together and discuss Scriptures related to the topic of the sketch the kids are learning. (Caution: A drama team is a ministry, but not an intensive spiritual training group. We require drama team members to be involved in a small group bible study as well as regularly attend Student Impact.) Give the team time together and when they feel secure, they will begin to share. It's the nature of the high-school beast not to want to be alone. When given a safe group, each member will break down his or her *own* walls.

Golden Rule Number Two

When you commit to the drama team, the commitment is for "whatever it takes."

"Whatever it takes" needs to be laid out specifically *before* auditions. Yes, it includes sticking to rehearsal schedules, even when that means missing out on other enticing activities. But it goes beyond practical dependability to include supporting and encouraging one another – helping others learn their lines, canceling plans to step in for a sick team member, comforting an actor who just blew his lines. "Whatever it takes" means that team members learn how to step outside themselves and think, "How can I be the most useful to the team and the ministry?" It means maturing.

Keep Their Feet on the Ground

Performing in front of a group of people is a buzz – hearing the audience laugh, applaud, go "Oooh" and "Ahhh." Being recognized and complimented does wonders for sagging self-esteem. That God-given kernel of self-worth can mutate, however; if not kept in check, terrific teens turn into Tasmanian Devils. Periodically warn your kids to beware the sly monster "Me-ism." We all need affirmation, but keep an eye open for ego disorders.

If you take the drama ministry seriously, your teens will gain a sense of importance and ministry ownership. The reach of their ministry will extend far beyond the impact of a cute little skit that fills time.

CHAPTER THREE

From Raw Recruits to Stage Stars

You: I've got the kids, I've got the performance date, I've got the script, and I've got an ulcer. What do I do now?

Us: You rehearse.

You: As in "read it through a couple of times"?

Us: As in ... well, pay attention, we'll tell you all about it.

You: You know, I'm getting to hate this chatting in the beginning of each section. Can't we just get on with it?

Us: Nah, we're having fun writing dialogue. It's our job, remember!

A glossary of terms generally accepted companies academically sophisticated books. Since we fall into that category (ahem), we decided to include one. But we have placed ours in the middle of the book, before we get into the format of the rehearsals, so that we can familiarize you with theater lingo. The following list of terms will aid you in your directing, expand your vocabulary, and most indubitably impress your team:

Actors – the ones who follow the director (and not the other way around).

Attack – how an actor starts his lines or enters the stage, with strength and purpose.

Blocking – telling the kids where to move throughout the sketch.

Delivery – how an actor says his lines.

Director – the one in charge, who makes final decisions.

Improv – making it up as you go along. (Great for rehearsals, pitiful for performances.)

Project – (pronounced with a long "o" and rolled "r") getting the voice out of the starting gate with the same power and deep breathing used to scream at a kid brother.

Set – the onstage props and objects and their placement.

Stage picture – freezing the scene (either in your mind or in actuality) at any point and evaluating whether the positions of the actors would make a good photograph. This is an easy way to check blocking for balance.

Stage positions –

	Upstage	
Stage Right	Center Stage	Stage Left
	Downstage	
	Audience	

(*Special note regarding stage positions:* The positions of actors on stage are spoken of from the perspective of the actor, not the audience. That is, "stage left" means to the actor's left, not the audience's left. If you are observing rehearsal from the audience position, your left is the actor's right. If you want an actor to move to the right [from your perspective] you have to say, "Move stage left." Note also that in days gone by, stages were built literally sloping up from the front to the back [like band risers]. Therefore, if an actor moved behind another actor, he would move upstage [up the slope]. Now it's usually the audience that sits on a sloped floor, and stages are flat. But the convention of stage position names remains.)

Structuring the Rehearsals

Because we performed a drama just about every time the youth group met, which was weekly, our rehearsal times were minimal but intense. We rehearsed for two or three hours four or five days before the performance, and then rehearsed on the stage area for two hours on the day of the performance. The actors were given the sketch about ten days before the performance. (Or as soon as we finished writing it! We were writing weekly as well.) The actors were expected to come to the first rehearsal with their lines memorized. Did you catch that? Lines memorized!

Here is a rough idea of how our rehearsals were structured. Our way is not the only way, but it is one example of the how-to's and to-do's of rehearsing.

Do warm-ups and play theater games. Since the kids usually arrived wound-up, we harnessed their energy through warm-up games. We might assign a role (biker, cheerleader, evangelist, suicidal teen) to one of the kids, and then have that kid take on the speech, manner, and movements suited to his character and improvise in front of the team. We worked on serious characters as well as humorous ones. And we often had the kids recite tongue twisters in different character voices and with different emotions. Dr. Seuss stories make terrific tongue twisters. Take your time on warm-ups. You are training your actors.

Work with the script. Have the team discuss their characters, each one telling about his or her character's likes, dislikes, relationships, positive and negative qualities. You may occasionally assign characters that the kids don't like. Discuss these characters' offensive qualities and then try to uncover some of their more positive aspects.

Then ask the students to go through the entire sketch sitting down – an exercise that brings the words to the forefront in their brains. Follow with work on blocking and delivery. The first few run-throughs of the sketch will be disastrous. The actors will overact, laugh at serious moments, and goof around. It's usually during the intensely emotional sketches that we get laugh attacks. You know the kind – every tragic line makes you laugh harder than the one before. This is nervousness. Let it come out – it will be much easier to get down to business if you do. But then do get down to business.

Getting down to business means developing blocking and delivery – that is, adding physical movement to the memorized dialogue. Lines are better remembered when they are linked with movement. No manual can explain the perfect blocking for theater. You can study basic techniques, but rely more on your intuition – on what movement feels natural and believable. Ask the actors to reflect the moods of their characters in the ways they stand, sit, use eye contact, hold their arms, walk, and breathe. Does the scene produced by the actors look staged or real?

Spiritual input. Allow time at the end

> **Getting down to business means developing blocking and delivery—that is, adding physical movement to the memorized dialogue.**

of rehearsals to share and pray together. We have found that if we begin our rehearsals with this quiet, reflective approach, the kids' energy vanishes and we waste valuable time trying to pump them up again to act.

Cancer Caution

Two degenerative diseases sweep through every team if not resisted: tardiness and careless script memorization. You'll be fighting these cancers throughout the life of the drama team. Expect them and continue to resist their decaying effects.

Giftedness

We are fully aware that the level of expectations we are presenting is high; excellence takes time and energy. But if your kids have a right gift fit, they will enjoy the process. If one or more kids fight your expectations or complain a lot, don't get angry at them. Drama may not be the area best suited to their gifts, and that's okay. Help them get involved in another area of service better matched to their abilities and passions. Serving in a ministry that matches our gifts doesn't seem like a drag because we are accomplishing the tasks God created us to enjoy. The Holy Spirit gives us all different abilities so that we can be different and unique

(1 Cor. 12). Then he gives us the fruit of the Spirit so we can use our differences to work together (Gal. 5:22-23).

* * * * *

You: Well, how do you direct the actors to move so that it doesn't look like a chess match?

Us: You start with motivation.

You: Oh, great! Now we have to give them a pep talk before we can rehearse?

Us: No. We're talking about that sophisticated, artsy motivation from within.

You: I think I'd rather give them a pep talk!

Motivation gives meaning to movement. Instead of planning out steps and turns, guide the actors to look into the sketch's emotion. Any movement needs to be connected to that emotion – feelings *guide* blocking. In "Scars," for example, Gwen moves away from Tony because she is afraid; her movement is needed to reflect the conflict between her affection for Tony and her terror of being touched.

An actor shouldn't stand or sit or turn away without good reason. Movement comes as an expression of feelings. If a character is angry, let that be the reason he turns away. If a character is frustrated, let that be the motivation for sitting down. If a character is nervous, let her have tight choppy movement. In everyday life, we move for reasons. It's exactly the same in theater. Try to be aware of how people move. Studying real life is excellent training for acting.

There are a number of sketches in this book in which overdone movements are necessary to carry off the sketch's intent ("Burning Up" and "Caterpillar Flight" are two examples). Exaggeration in voice and movement enhance their presentation.

Right in line with proper motivation is a technique called "playing against the emotion." During a powerful dramatic moment, for example, kids tend to overact – to overact the anger, the sadness, the joy. In real life, however, most people try to cover up their honest feelings by showing safer emotions.

Take the guy who feels affection for a girl, as an example. Does he tell her how he feels? Fat chance. He teases her. But if we look closely, tenderness sneaks out in unexpected ways. If a jock is scared, how does he express it? He hurts someone in an angry fit, rather than to admit to being afraid. But again, if we look deeply, we will see some of his fear leaking through the macho facade. That is real life.

That's what we want to see in drama rather than melodramatics. Playing against the emotion is not a lack of emotion; it is rather guarding strong feelings lest they show, internalizing them. Read "Turn Around is Fair Play," keeping the concept of "playing against the emotion" in the forefront of your mind. Then read it again imagining how it would look if played melodramatically. See the difference? We hope so.

Go with Your Intuition

Trying to describe something as subjective as intuition is difficult, but intuition is a key element in any creative art. Directors as well as actors have to listen to their gut feelings. Using intuition means going beyond the words you hear to the feelings you experience while watching the drama – and then trusting those feelings enough to let them guide your direction. Evaluate a sketch intuitively by asking questions: "How do I feel about this drama? Do I like it? Is it believable or does it feel overacted and unrealistic? Does this drama evoke any authentic emotions in me? Do I feel in any way connected to what is being dramatized?" If an actor is facing left and you sense that something is wrong, experiment – move people and even props around until you can say, "That's it – that's what I want!" Ask yourself over and over: "Do I believe this?" Work at the sketch until you can say, "Yes! This is like real life."

For those of you who need something more objective, try critiquing sitcoms on television. As you watch, note how frequently and naturally the actors move. Television uses a variety of camera angles as well blocking techniques to vary scenes. Since there are no fluctuating camera angles in live drama, concentrate on the actors' body movements. Note when, why, and how the actors sit. Where do they look when they are speaking? What are the actors not in the limelight doing? We love watching the actors who are out of the focal point. It's amazing how much energy goes into background acting. You know you've witnessed good acting when a scene feels believable.

And now for a few objective blocking tips:

- *The audience likes to see face cheeks, not the other kind.* Keep backs to the back (upstage).
- *Don't let actors stand in front of each other.* Blocked blocking will block the scene, blockhead!
- *Arrange the actors in angles and arches* rather than straight lines.
- *Have actors attack their entrances and exits* instead of fading on and offstage.
- *Allow actors to give advice, but only to the director,* not to other actors. It is overwhelming to have five people

directing at the same time. Stay in control.
- *Adjust any words and phrases which an actor finds uncomfortable or difficult to say.* Adjusting the scripts is fine ... well, maybe some parts ... that is to say, a few words here or there ... or at most, one or two words ... all right, forget we even brought it up.
- *Rehearse, rehearse, rehearse.*
- *Over and over and over.*

* * * * *

You: This is great. I've got my actors moving with feeling yet "playing against the emotion," unless the sketch is melodramatic, in which case I let them whack out and overact.

Us: Is that what we said?

You: Well, maybe not the "whack out" part.

Us: Whew, we were scared! But notice how we played against the emotion by asking a calm, somewhat factual question. Our actual feelings were more of, "Where the heck did you come up with that? We've been misquoted! The next thing you know we'll have a lawsuit on our hands because someone got hurt by something someone else said we said but we really didn't say!"

You: Are you two usually this para-

noid?
Us: No, no. Of course not.
You: Playing against the emotion?
Us: Uh … let's move on … quickly.

Naturally, if emotions are to guide movement, the actors need to project verbally what they are feeling. This is called "delivery" (see definition list earlier in this chapter. It has nothing to do with U.P.S. or what happens in maternity wards.) Just as we need to train our bodies to act, we need to train our voices to communicate. There are two fundamentals to delivery: getting it said, and getting it heard.

Getting It Said

Use tongue twisters to warm up vocal cavities (see appendix for material).
Practice exaggerated enunciation – pronouncing every <u>consonant</u> in a <u>word</u>.
Practice volume and pitch variations (loud, soft, high pitch, low pitch, and everything in between).
Use Psalms as material to practice expressing emotion.

Getting It Heard

It all comes down to this folks – if the audience can't hear what the actors are saying, then your work is wasted. What good are great costumes, terrific act-ing, wonderful blocking, and breathtaking scenery, if the audience hears only mumbles?

If you will be playing for small groups, rehearse in the room where you'll perform in order to test the volume. Remember, bodies absorb sound, so when the room is filled, the sound won't carry as well. If your audience is larger, a microphone system is a must. Through practice the actors will learn how close they have to be to the microphones in order to be heard. Actors commonly come to the wrong conclusion that because they are being miked, they no longer have to project. *Baloney!* Actors always have to project. Miking enhances the sound that is there; it doesn't create it. If you don't already have access to equipment and a knowledgeable technician, ask around in the congregation and see if there is an adult who has sound equipment and might be willing to be your sound person. Eventually, with experience and training, one of your student team members might be able to move into that position.

> It all comes down to this folks—if the audience can't hear what the actors are saying, then your work is wasted.

And now for the "sting." One of the most effective methods for getting actors serious about what they are doing is to videotape. Film a sketch during a complete run-through at rehearsal. (If you videotape an actual performance, be sure it isn't distracting to the drama team or the audience.) Then let them watch it together and critique it. They will learn about believability when they see it working … or not working. But please focus on only one or two things for each actor to work on. Too much input will be overwhelming.

The Stages of Staging

One of the most relieving consolations about drama is that you don't have to have millions of dollars to pull it off! (A couple of K maybe, but not millions.) Actually we have operated for as little as twenty-five dollars a month, and that was doing a sketch every week. As far as sets are concerned, the old adage applies: "Less is more." Here's a handy step-by-step guide to help you construct sets and collect needed paraphernalia without breaking the youth ministry's budget:

Select a focal point. Somewhere in the place you are meeting, create a stage area and separate it from the audience by at least four feet. Select a focal point that is not surrounded by distractions. When there are other things to look at, the audience will look at them. When the audience is not distracted, they will see only what you want them to see.

Force concentration by accenting the stage area. Use lights. Turn them on when the performance begins and turn them off when the performance ends. (We know this is basic. We were told to write very basic. So we write basic.) Get an electrician from your church to help make some spotlights out of coffee cans and run them up a pole. Aim the lights at the actors (not the stage) and you will have forced audience concentration. Use a raised stage. Plywood panels on wooden frames that lift the actors six inches off the ground force concentration. Build burlap-covered frames (about eight feet high) that fold like shutters for each side of the stage area. These will set apart the stage area, even if you don't have lights and sets, and will also give the actors a place from which to enter and exit and behind which to hide, if necessary.

Most of your costumes can come from the teams' bedroom closets since the sketches are contemporary. If you need clothing, frequent garage sales and resale shops. When more unusual costumes are needed, such as those required for "Caterpillar Flight," stylize. The suggestion of a costume is more effective than a low-budget, elaborate costume. Green pants, green turtlenecks, cardboard footprints attached to small springs and taped on the front of the caterpillar's body, and springs with balls on the ends for antennae are what we used for the costume.

Follow the same principle for props as for costuming: Keep things simple. Three chairs butted up side by side make a satisfactory couch. Cardboard painted to look like the front of two or three lockers will give the illusion of a school hall or locker room. Depending on the table covering or accessories used, a folding table can become a desk, a kitchen table, or a cafeteria table. Chairs in rows become a classroom. The suggestion of a scene is more effective than a full, elaborate set. Feel free to mime interactions with bathroom mirrors, cars, books, or phones. The less props you use, the less you have to remember to find, and the less chance you have of not getting them on stage when they are needed.

It's our hope that you will use with genuine enthusiasm what God has provided for your drama team and not think that you have to wait until you have sets and costumes equal to Disney World's before you perform. We relish simplicity.

* * * * *

It's Show Time!

You: You mean that's all the help you're going to give me? You can't just leave me. These kids are going to get up in front of everyone in the world, and if it's lousy, *I'm* the one who'll lose my head!

Us: We know the church has a tendency to be a bit behind the times, but the chopping block went out of vogue centuries ago. Besides, we're not abandoning you. We've got more to give. You know, you might want to look into some therapy … seems like you've got an abandonment issue there.

You: Well, I do remember when I was five that I was really attached to an aunt and she moved to …

Us: Uh … some other time, please.

You: Oh, sorry.

You know, it's not crucial that you find out everything there is to know before you start. God has obviously given you a passion for drama or you wouldn't be reading this book. And God promises to equip you for a task when he calls you to do it. Granted, he may not give you all you need before you begin. But some of the adventure of Christian theater is trying and learning and messing up and succeeding and trying some more and learning and being humbled and seeing kids grow, and yes, impossible as it seems, seeing yourself grow. Quoting a friend, "God hasn't called me to change the world. All he calls me to do is be faithful." And faithfulness encompasses working with as much excellence as we can muster, believing in our calling, and trusting the One who calls. Now on with the show ...

In sports, what's the one principle every coach pounds into his players' heads? You can say it in a word – fundamentals. Keep your eye on the ball, don't move until the ball does, watch your stance, concentrate, never let them see you sweat (maybe that one is from a deodorant commercial). Fundamentals exist in theater as well – little phrases that can be uttered time and time again to help each performance be top notch.

Attack – give purpose to your entrances and exits.
Remember the stage picture.
Project.
Watch your pace (the tendency of bodies filled with adrenaline is to go either very fast or painstakingly slow).
Project.
Don't break character – for the entire time you are on stage, be the character; if you forget a line or move the wrong way, keep going; improvise if needed, but stay in character.
Project (Have we mentioned that already?).
Pray.

After the Curtain Falls

As soon as they get offstage, your performers will be buzzing, laughing, crying, expressing anger, embarrassment, and relief. As the director, your opinion will be the one most respected. Be encouraging. Even if the performance falls apart, find something positive to say. The kids deserve your commendations.

In addition to encouragement, you need to offer valid criticism. Be honest, yet sensitive. It is very damaging to tell someone they did an okay job when their performance actually stunk. Gentle honesty is what we owe each other, not cloaked, half-truths (see "The Deception of Diane").

It's a good idea to gather a few other adults who have a good eye for theater to be *your* critics as well. You need building up and support to keep your passion flamed. Their eyes can keep your vision from clouding.

So that's some of what it takes to be a director. By completing the last three chapters, you have learned the difference between an air-bag and an air-head. And you are neither. Congratulations!

CHAPTER FOUR

How to Take Full Advantage of These Sketches

*I*f we could emphasize any one concept when using *Super Sketches* it would be this: "Drama is to show, not tell." These sketches are designed to

avoid teachy-ness, preachy-ness, knock-the-kids-over-the-head-with-the-right-answer-ness! We offer sketches that will present a conflict (often without a complete resolution). These sketches will open the door for the topic of the meeting. Then the rest of your program brings the subject matter to the conclusion you're aiming for.

These sketches each last about ten minutes (unless the actors really screw up and have to start

over). We are aware that most youth group meetings last a bit longer than that. So we'd like to offer some suggestions for what to do with the rest of the meeting.

The Student Impact formula is to decide in advance the focus of a message or series of messages. The sketches in this book are arranged topically because we wrote them that way. As you choose your topic (dating, family, or values, for example), the per-

son in charge of music should look for contemporary songs, the drama person should find or create a sketch, and the youth minister should prepare a message, all focused on that chosen subject. Our program usually goes like this:

- Opening music number – the wilder, the better
- Announcements and introduction to topic of meeting
- Drama
- Mellow music number
- Message

Our music is live. If this is impossible in your situation, good recordings played over a quality system will work.

Our youth pastor is a teacher and an evangelist. He uses his gifts to address the questions of today's teens and give answers from God's perspective. Your speaker doesn't need to get caught up in trying to toss out simplified answers like pieces of candy. Cut and dried, unfeeling answers are usually discarded as trash by a teen's mind. It is more important in these talks to take risks and expose heartfelt emotions. As the speaker prepares, he or she must ask some difficult questions: What do *I* really feel and believe about the topic? What aspects of the subject have ever been or even now are difficult for me to deal with personally? The speaker's openness and respect for those listening will sink into hearts. Sometimes it adds to your presentation to invite in an outside speaker. Topics like sexual abuse and suicide are best handled by someone with the appropriate qualifications.

Every subject you choose does not have to plumb the depths of teen despair. Aim most often for students who are well-adjusted but who still need Christ. But when you do handle the tough issues, please be prepared. At those times you will be inviting teens to open up their infected wounds. Be ready to spend the time it will take to offer the Lord's healing for hurting kids. Don't underestimate the intensity of their pain. Equip yourself with references to professionals qualified to help kids – or have an expert on hand. An "I can handle these kids' problems – I had a psychology class in school" attitude will not do justice to their needs.

More Ways to Use These Sketches

- We've included discussion questions with each sketch. Depending on the size and flavor of your youth group, these questions can be used as springboards for small-group interaction. Individuals may share more honestly in groups of three to five than in a larger group setting. On a few of the more sensitive sketches, we've recommended dividing the groups by gender. Work to create an environment that encourages openness. Each set of questions also draws attention to a related Bible passage that reinforces God's involvement in these contemporary issues.

• Don't push to do a sketch a week at the beginning. Take your time. Invest yourself in the drama team. Do the sketches with as much excellence as possible. Quantity is not as critical as quality.

• Use the drama team as an idea group for planning future meetings. Coming up with ideas can be as fulfilling as executing them.

• These sketches work well as part of a teen Sunday service. Use your best dramas – a quality production will both touch the congregation and add to the credibility of your youth program.

• Once your team is established and has a repertoire from which to work, consider sending them out to other church youth groups as a ministry of evangelism and encouragement. You'll be amazed at how responsible teens can be when given an opportunity like this.

Drama as Discipleship

We've observed the effects of quality Christian drama from the vantage points of both actor and audience. We know how lives will be changed as you

use it. Teens will gain a new appreciation for Christ and His care, love, and involvement in their lives. They will see that God is not old, outdated, and out-of-touch, but that He is with them right in the center of their adolescent universe.

Timothy was a young believer discipled by Paul. We find the letters to Timothy have many applications for the director/drama team relationship. "But you, keep your head in all situations," Paul exhorts in 2 Timothy 4:5, "endure hardship, do the work of an evangelist, discharge all the duties of your ministry."

"Keep your head in all situations ..."

For you:
You will be watched, scrutinized, and imitated. Drama is not always a breeze. Kids will not live up to your expectations all the time. Keep the ministry in perspective. Remember to allow the kids to be kids. Allow yourself to feel all the frustration, joy, worry, and affection that come from this type of ministry, but guard your mind and heart. Keep your head, no matter what, when you are

> You will be watched, scrutinized, and imitated. Drama is not always a breeze. Kids will not live up to your expectations all the time.

functioning as the director.

For the team:
You will be living in a fishbowl. You will be imitated, criticized, envied. We don't expect perfection, but foolishness is damaging. Keep your head in all situations.

" ... endure hardships ..."

For you:
If God has led you to this ministry, expect resistance from Satan. Expect setbacks and disappointments – maybe even a disaster or two. If you don't have difficulties, you are probably not threatening anyone.

For the team:
Life is not fair – neither are all the decisions made by your director. You will not always get what you want. Respectfully express your feelings, but then cooperate. You will blow your lines, you will be pressured at times trying to balance school, work, and the drama team. The issue is not *will* it happen, but how will you respond *when* it happens.

" ... do the work of an evangelist ..."

For you:
Live an exemplary evangelistic lifestyle. Let your team see that you care about the lost. Though you are involved in acting, show that real life – every real person without Christ – matters to you, too.

For the team:
All believers are required to do evangelism, not just those with the specific gift. The primary goal of the kind of drama program we've written about in *Super Sketches* is to draw nonbelievers into a deeper understanding of a God who really cares, relates, and helps. Encouragement and challenge will happen for believers through drama, but we especially want to concentrate on those who do not know Christ.

" ... discharge all the duties of your ministry."

For you and the team:
The duties of a drama ministry are servanthood, godliness, faithfulness, patience ... and excellent drama. Paul did not offer these points as suggestions to Timothy. They were orders. We cannot look at this verse as offering helpful guidelines only. It gives specific instructions to be followed.

We long for you to experience the joy and satisfaction of developing a quality teen drama team. We have witnessed the remarkable impact of drama in teen's lives. When Deb recently visited a church in another town, a beautiful young woman excitedly approached her. "I'm so glad you're here," she bubbled. "Wait until you see the drama." After a few embarrassing moments, Deb remembered that this married, pregnant woman was a mature version of never-sit-still-bouncing-laughing-lovable-willing-to-do-anything Tracy, a member of her youth drama team from eight years earlier.

"I was filled with wonder and thankfulness," Deb recalls, "as I watched Tracy act with the adult drama team for the Sunday morning service. She was great! She was gifted! She was a vital force in that church's drama ministry. And she was reaching many with Christ's message of understanding, forgiveness, and hope. Granted, I felt older seeing one of my kids all grown up. But this reality of passing years was delightful and very rewarding."

God's creativity is never ending. His resources are unlimited. His passion for nonbelievers to know him is unquenchable. His desire for believers to mature is unceasing. And he will use his power and creativity and us to get this done. And high school Christian drama is part of that wild, wonderful process.

* * * * *

Deb: Well Sharon, we'd better end this. Got any creative ideas?

Sharon: Come on, Deb. You know I'm not good at endings.

Deb: Yeah, I know. And the ones I come up with usually stink.

Sharon: What about quoting Red Skelton? "Good night, and may God bless."

Deb: Too cutesy. What about pulling our ears like Carol?

Sharon: And how are they going to see that?

Deb: Oh. Hey, I've got an idea.

Sharon: Are you thinking along the same lines I am?

Deb: And-a-one, and-a-two …

Us: (*singing*) Onward Christian thespians, book of scripts in tow, Trusting that these chapters have all that you must know …

You: (*interrupting*) It's God's grace you two never became song writers!

PART TWO

Scripts

I first came to the
youth group about a
year ago. I wasn't
interested in God, but I came
because a friend invited me.
I don't remember what the
message was that first time, but I
do remember the drama. I'll
never forget how weird it was to
see someone acting out just how
I was feeling. I kept coming back,
mainly to see the drama, and
eventually began hearing the
message. I'm a Christian now."
—Valerie

Christ in Our Lives

SECRET AGENT ANDY

Debra J. Poling

Characters

Andy high school student, new Christian, but hides it by not telling his friends. He wears a trench coat and a hat covering his eyes.

Dave Andy's best friend, high school student

Pam Andy's friend, high school student

Joy Andy's friend, high school student

*The scene is a hallway at school just after an algebra exam. **Dave**, **Pam**, and **Joy** enter. **Andy** enters last. He walks very nervously, as if someone is following him.*

Pam: I can't believe ol' Pencil-Brain Peabody really expected us to be able to finish that exam in fifty minutes!

Joy: He doesn't know the first thing about teaching.

Dave: I bet nobody passed ... except Gertrude!

Joy: Yeah. But I'd rather be in touch with reality and not get straight A's than be like Gertrude.

Dave: (*imitating* **Gertrude**, *a brainy geek*) Now girls, I don't think you should talk about Mr. Peabody like that. He is a very intelligent man. (**All** *laugh except* **Andy**.)

Pam: What's wrong with you, Andy? Don't you think Dave's imitation of Gertrude is funny?

Andy: (*mumbling*) Ah, it was okay.

Dave: Just okay? Hey, you like Peabody or something?

Andy: (*mumbling*) He's okay.

Joy: (*loudly, shocked*) He's okay? Come on, Andy, you don't really believe that, do you?

Andy: (*mumbling*) I just don't think we should make fun of other people.

Pam: Hey, Andy ... didn't you think the test was hard?

Andy: It was okay.

Dave: I bet you did really good on it, didn't you?

Pam: Yeah, you've been turning kinda weird on us lately. I bet you studied all day Saturday and Sunday.

Andy: (*defensively*) I did not! I didn't study at all Sunday morning. I wasn't even home!

Joy: Where were you?

Andy: Ah ... ah, I ... I just wasn't home.

Dave: Come on, Andy, where were you? We're your friends.

Pam: I bet he was lying drunk on a street somewhere.

Andy: I was not!

Joy: Well then, where were you?

Andy: Never mind.

Dave: Come on, Pam, let's get out of here. I'm tired of all this secret stuff. (*to* **Andy**) Some friend. Won't even tell his best friend what he did on the weekend. (**Dave** *leaves*)

Pam: Bye, Andy ... or should I say, Secret Agent Andy! (*leaves laughing*)

Joy: Bye, you guys. (*to* **Andy**) What's gotten into you lately? Dave is really ticked at you for being so secretive about your life.

Andy: Oh yeah? Like what?

Joy: For starters, what about last Thursday when you didn't show up for his wrestling meet?

Andy: I had other plans.

Joy: What plans?

Andy: Never mind.

Joy: See, that's exactly what I mean. You can't keep friends and not tell them what you're doing.

Andy: I know.

Joy: So, what are you doing that you won't tell anybody?

Andy: Joy, you gotta promise not to tell a soul.

Joy: Andy, what kind of trouble are you in?

Andy: Just promise you won't tell anyone. Promise?

Joy: Sure Andy ... my lips are sealed.

Andy: Well, here goes ... the whole truth ... Joy, three weeks ago I ... I ... I –

Joy: You ... you ... you ... what?

Andy: I can't say it. You'll never want to be near me again.

Joy: (*almost screaming*) Andy, what did you do?

Andy: (*screaming back*) I became a Christian! (*realizing he's yelling, pulls his hat way down over his face*)

Joy: (*shocked*) You became a Christian?

Andy: Yes. Now you promised not to tell anyone.

Joy: And that's where you've been on Sunday mornings?

Andy: (*embarrassed and ashamed*) Yes, yes, that's the truth! Oh, I'm so embarrassed.

Joy: Andy, why are you embarrassed?

Andy: Because now everyone will think I'm weird and start making fun of me like they do of Gertrude.

Joy: I don't know exactly what it means to become a Christian, but if something important has happened to you, then why wouldn't you just tell us?

Andy: Well, I thought you'd see it in the way I lived.

Joy: The way you lived? You mean in hiding?

Andy: I thought if I got good grades and was nice to people that pretty soon someone would know I was doing it because I was a Christian.

Joy: Andy, Gertrude gets good grades and nobody thinks she's doing it for God. I think it's very interesting what's happened to you.

Andy: You do? And you don't think I'm weird?

Joy: I think you're weird for wearing that coat and hat and hiding.

Andy: I guess I do look pretty stupid.

Joy: Yeah, why don't you take that stuff off?

Andy: (*taking off his coat and hat*) Yeah … okay.

Joy: And take off the mask you're wearing about being a Christian, too.

Andy: You really don't think people will think I'm weird for getting into God?

Joy: Look, I don't know what others will think. Dave will probably bug you about it. But you can't keep hiding it from him.

Andy: You're right.

Dave: (*enters with **Pam***) Hey, Andy, you took off that stupid hat and coat.

Andy: (*looking up*) Give me strength. (*to* **Dave**) Hi, Dave. Hey, there's something I gotta tell you.

Dave: I don't believe it ... Mr. Secret Agent is going to talk to his old buddy. What's up?

Andy: (*whispers to* **Dave**)

Dave: (*shocked*) You became a what!?!

Andy: (*dragging* **Dave** *offstage*) Dave, let's go some place alone and talk about it.

Dave: (*on the way offstage*) You did what?

Pam: (*exiting with* **Joy**) Joy, what did he do ... what did he do?

Discussion Questions

1. Have you ever talked to someone about your own relationship with Christ? What was their reaction?
2. What do you think most people who aren't Christians think of those who are? Why ?
3. What is one of the worst things one of your non-Christian friends could say or do to you if you talked about your faith? What would you do if your fear actually came true?
4. Some Christians are vocal about their relationships with God, while some never want to speak up. Where do you put yourself along that continuum? Where would you like to be?
5. Jesus said, "But whoever disowns me before men, I will disown him before my Father in heaven" (Matt. 10:33). What do you think he meant by that? Why would he put such value on talking openly about him?

WHAT BATTLE?

Debra J. Poling

Characters

Tim high school senior

Gabriel veteran guardian angel, dressed in white clothes, calm, mature, training Angelina

Angelina angel-in-training, also wearing white.

Sledgehog cocky demon, evil "Fonzy" type, in black clothes.

Wartnose same as Sledgehog

Tim *is sitting at his desk doing calculus in his bedroom. He is totally unaware of the angels and demons around him.* **Angelina** *and* **Gabriel** *are standing about six feet behind him to stage right. Most of the interaction between the angels and demons takes place behind Tim.*

Gabriel: I'm glad Tim finally settled down to do his calculus.

Angelina: Yeah. Reminding him about his dad's threat to take away car privileges if he got any more D's worked great.

Gabriel: Tim's a good kid. He just gets sidetracked easily.

Angelina: I bet that's why the Chief assigned two of us to watch over him, instead of just one. (*enter* **Sledgehog** *and* **Wartnose** – *stage left*) Uh-oh, Gabriel, looks like we've got trouble.

Gabriel: Don't panic. Let them make the first move.

Sledgehog: Hey, Tim, ya bookworm. What'cha slaving over that stupid math for?

Wartnose: You'll never use it for nothin'. (**Tim** *looks up for a second, then goes back to his work.*)

Sledgehog: Isn't your teacher that lousy Ms. Krantz? She's not worth doing homework for.

Wartnose: Remember how she embarrassed you in front of

the whole class last year?

Sledgehog: She gave you a lower grade just because you had rotten handwriting.

Wartnose: It's not your fault she can't see through those coke bottles she calls glasses. (**Tim** *puts his pencil down and looks angry as he remembers the incident.*)

Sledgehog: Now just take that assignment and throw it in her face! (**Tim** *picks up the paper as if ready to crumple it up.*)

Angelina: We gotta do something!

Gabriel: Just follow me. Tim, picture your college entrance exams showing a big zero in the math score. You're not doing your homework for Krantz, but for yourself and your future.

Angelina: Yeah, Krantz isn't going to be around forever, but you'll have to live with your successes and failures your whole life. (**Tim**

picks up his pencil and starts working again.)

Gabriel: Nice job, Angel.

Angelina: Very convincing yourself, Gabe.

(**Gabriel** *and* **Angelina** *proudly watch* **Tim**. **Sledgehog** *and* **Wartnose** *are pacing, angry at the loss of this battle. Suddenly* **Sledgehog** *gets an idea and signals* **Wartnose** *to watch him.*)

Sledgehog: *Susan!*

(*Instantly* **Tim** *drops his pencil and melts his chin into the heels of his hands. His mind has totally forgotten calculus.*)

Angelina: That's not fair! They're playing dirty.

Gabriel: What do you expect?

Angelina: We'll never get Tim back once Susan enters his mind.

Wartnose: What a night Friday was. She was putty in your hands. (**Tim** *sighs.*)

Sledgehog: Just wait 'til the guys hear about your conquest.

Gabriel: Conquest? My, how quickly our memories fade. Obviously much quicker than bruised cheeks heal from being slapped by sweet little putty-in-your-hands Susan.

Sledgehog: (*Defensively to* **Gabriel** *... this is the first time the angels and demons interact.*) She was just being playful.

Gabriel: (*to* **Sledgehog**) Liar! (*to* **Tim**, *firmly*) Now get your head out of the clouds and finish your homework!

Wartnose: Forget the homework. Susan doesn't want to date an egghead.

Gabriel: She won't date an empty head, either!

(*The* **demons** *and* **angels** *stare angrily at each other for a moment, then each side breaks into a brief huddle. They turn and face each other as if to start a tag team all-star wrestling match. During this section the* **angels** *and* **demons** *throw each other around as they say their lines.*)

Angelina: If you get your homework done you'll be able to watch Monday Night Football. (**Angelina** *pushes* **Sledgehog** *over.*)

Sledgehog: (*getting up and then throwing* **Angelina**) Who cares about football? The Bears are doing lousy anyway.

Gabriel: (*helping* **Angelina** *get on her feet*) Come on, get up, Angelina. We've just begun the battle. (*crossing to* **Wartnose**) Wartnose, Tim is getting better at recognizing when you and Sledgehog are bugging him.

Wartnose: He dropped his pencil awfully quickly when I said just one word – *Susan*! (**Tim** *stops working to think about Susan again.*)

Gabriel: And he started working with only a short reminder of the truth. (**Gabriel** *flings* **Wartnose** – **Tim** *begins working again.*)

Angelina: You creeps gotta stop hanging around Tim.

(**All four** *enter into an all-out brawl as they say the following lines.* **Tim** *is totally unaware of what is going on throughout all of this.*)

Wartnose: You don't let him have fun anymore.

Gabriel: You think fun is getting wasted and arrested.

Sledgehog: You're right! The more trouble, the better.

Angelina: If you'd leave him alone, he wouldn't want anything to do with you.

Wartnose: That's exactly why we will *not* leave him alone.

Angelina: What did you say?

(*They all stop fighting.*)

Wartnose: We know Tim doesn't want anything to do with us.

Sledgehog: We know Tim belongs to your Chief.

Angelina: You know you've lost him? Why don't you just let him be?

Gabriel: They won't leave him alone because –

Sledgehog: Gabe, allow me. (*to **Angelina***) We know a lot more than you think. In the end Tim is going to have to explain his life to your Chief.

Wartnose: (*evilly*) And if we can make that life a failure, then, although we lost Tim, we gain a wasted life.

Gabriel: And so they fight us, and will continue to fight us until the Chief puts an end to the battle.

Wartnose: Ah, nuts, Sledgehog, Tim is finishing his homework.

Sledgehog: (*angrily to **Gabriel***) You won this round. But we'll be back … count on it. (**Wartnose** *and* **Sledgehog** *exit*)

Angelina: Man, I've got a lot to learn.

Gabriel: And Tim has a lot to learn also. Come on, we've got to keep an eye on those two. (*exit to follow* **Wartnose** *and* **Sledgehog**)

Tim: (*finishing the last question*) There, I'm finally done with this stupid assignment. (*closing his book,* **Tim** *stands to leave.*) Another night at home with nothing going on. I wonder when the Christian life will get some action and excitement in it?

Discussion Questions

1. What do you think angels are like? What about demons? How much influence do you think they have on the visible world? What kind of influence?
2. If you could describe an area of your life in which there seems to be an invisible battle going on, what would it be?
3. What effect do you think prayer has on the invisible world of angels and demons?
4. If you were a demon, how would you try to wreck your (current human) life?
5. If you were an angel, how would you try to help your (current human) life?
6. Why do you think Jesus had so much contact with demons during his ministry? Do you think they're still active today? If so, how?

THE MISSING PEACE

Sharon Sherbondy

Characters
Margaret   middle-aged mother
Howard   middle-aged father
Tim   senior in high school

Stage is set as living room. **Margaret** *is straightening up the couch.* **Howard** *walks in.*

Margaret: Well, hi, Honey. You're home a little early today.

Howard: Well, I decided to put some projects on hold at work in order to get an early start on our weekend.

Margaret: Why, are we doing something special?

Howard: No, I just thought it would be a good weekend for you and the kids and me to spend some time together.

Margaret: Oh, how thoughtful. But I'll tell you who I think really needs some attention and that's Tim.

Howard: Tim? What's the matter with him?

Margaret: That's just it. I don't know. He's been acting so unlike himself lately.

Howard: Well, he has been a little quieter, but it's probably due to the decisions he's got to make about college and his future. Being a senior –

Margaret: Howard, I think it's more than that. (*looks around.* **Howard** *mimics her, puzzled.*) I'm wondering if he's got some girl in trouble.

Howard: Margaret! Our son, Tim?

Margaret: Now, Howard, he *is* at that age. And I'm telling you, he's been acting very strangely.

Howard: Well, no son of mine had better do anything of the sort. Where is he? We're going to talk about this right here and now.

Margaret: He's in his room. But, dear, be gentle with the boy. Remember, you were young once.

Howard: That was different. Tim! Tim, come down here.

Margaret: Now, Howard, don't do anything rash. They're going to need our help.

Howard: (*hitting his fist in the other hand*) They're going to need help, all right. Tim, come down here, now!

Tim: Yeah, Dad? I'm right here. What's up?

Howard: You sit down, young man.

Tim: What's the matter? Did I do something?

Howard: Why don't you tell me?

Tim: Tell you what?

Howard: All right, we'll play it your way. Let's start with her name.

Tim: Whose name?

Howard: The girl, Tim. Who's the girl?

Tim: Oh, you mean Melissa. She's just a girl I know from school.

Howard: Know is right. Like Adam *knew* Eve.

Tim: What?

Margaret: Tim, your father and I are willing to help, but you need to start being honest with us.

Tim: What are you talking about?

Howard: Come on, Tim. We weren't born yesterday and we're not dumb. We know you got the girl pregnant.

Tim: (*jumps up and chokes and screams*) What?!

Howard: You heard me. The cards are on the table now, boy.

Tim: Dad, I don't know what you're talking about.

Margaret: Tim, there's no need to lie anymore.

Tim: I'm not lying. Where'd you get such an off-the-wall idea?!

Howard: (*awkwardly*) Well, your mother ... Margaret?

Margaret: Well, Tim, I just thought ... I mean, you've been acting so strange and withdrawn. I just thought –

Tim: Well, you can stop thinking. I can't believe my own parents ...

Howard: Your mother. It was your mother, Son. Margaret, for heaven's sake. We brought our son up with more sense than that. How you get carried away with things.

Margaret: Me carried away! You're the one ... oh, never mind.

Howard: Well, Son, what's the problem then? Your mother was right about one thing – you haven't been yourself lately.

Tim: I know.

Margaret: Tim, dear, we'd like to help if we can. Just tell us what's on your mind.

Tim: I don't know. I've just been doing a lot of thinking lately.

Howard: About what?

Tim: Life.

Margaret: Now, Tim, like your father said earlier, we know it's tough being a senior, but worrying isn't going to help you make the decision about college and who you're going to ask to the prom ...

Tim: Mom, it's more than that. I just feel like something's missing in my life, but I don't know what.

Howard: Well, I certainly don't know what it would be, either. We've bought you your own car, TV, compact disc ...

Margaret: You've got yourself a little girlfriend – what's her name? Melissa? And more friends than I can keep track of.

Howard: We've given you a good home and a roof over your head.

Margaret: Food and love.

Tim: I know. I know. It doesn't have anything to do with you. I've got everything I could ever need or want.

Howard: Well, then what is it?

Tim: I don't know. (*pause*) I'm about to graduate from high school …

Margaret: And we're so proud of you.

Tim: And I'm headed for college to spend four years of my life preparing for my future. Why?

Howard: Why? Well, Tim, that's the craziest question I've ever heard. Why else? To make something of yourself. To have security and stability, not to mention a steady income.

Tim: That's what I mean. Security, stability, and money coming from working eight to fifteen hours a day. What kind of life is that?

Howard: Well, it's a darn good one. It's made a good life for your mother and me – plus, I've never heard you complain.

Tim: But there's got to be more. It just doesn't seem like enough. Dad, I don't mean to cut down you or everything you've worked for, but it just seems to me that there's got to be something more to life than getting up in the morning, eating breakfast, going to work, coming home, eating dinner, watching TV, going to bed, then doing it all over again.

Margaret: Don't forget our two-week vacations every year.

Howard: So you think you can do things better?

Tim: No, Dad, that's not what I'm saying.

Howard: Say, have you been hanging around some of those weirdos at school? Is that who's putting these crazy ideas in your head? Because if you are ...

Tim: No, Dad. In fact, I've been doing just the opposite. I've been spending time with some kids who seem to have it all together – or at least seem to have some meaning and purpose in their lives.

Howard: That's just what it looks like on the outside. Take it from your old dad – nobody has "got it all together" as you call it. Listen, this is it. There is nothing else. And you're just wasting your time and energy looking for a solution.

Margaret: Your father's right, dear. Besides, you're still very young. It's too early in life for you to be thinking such thoughts. You'll have plenty of time to think when you're our age.

Tim: But I don't want to wait. I can't wait. There's something missing in my life, and I've got to find out what it is.

Howard: Tim, I think I understand what you're after. I used to think the same way. But let me give you some advice. I'm older and I've lived longer than you, and I've found that at times like this when you come across these kind of questions, it's easier just not to think about it. This is all there is, Tim, and the sooner you start accepting that the better off you'll be.

Tim: No offense, Dad, but I'm just not going to settle for a routine, mediocre life. I know there's more because of those friends I was telling you about. Maybe it's God, I don't know. They talk about him a lot.

Howard: Here now, let's not go off the deep end.

Tim: Dad, I've gotta go some-where – anywhere that will get me out of this shallowness I'm stuck in.

Margaret: Say, I've got an idea! Why don't we just forget about all this depressing talk and go out and have us a big juicy pizza? We'll talk about college and girls and our next vacation. You know where I'd like to go – Washington, D.C. Doesn't that sound like fun? And it'd be educational.

Tim: No, thanks, Mom. You and Dad go. I'm not very hungry.

Howard: Tim, we'll talk more about this later. (**Tim** exits.) He's got to learn the hard way, Margaret. He'll find out sooner or later that it's just a lot easier not to think about it.

Discussion Questions
1. What could Dad or Mom have done differently to help Tim?
2. What do you think Tim is looking for?
3. When you have similar questions, whom do you talk to? Why?
4. What's it like to talk to your parents about spiritual matters?
5. How can you "let your light shine"?

JACK AND THE VINE

Sharon Sherbondy

Characters

Mother   poorly dressed, middle-aged woman

Jack   teenage son

Giant

Banqueters elegantly dressed

At right a banquet table is set with dishes, platters, glasses, candles, centerpiece, etc. At left are two chairs.

Mother: (*sweeping the floor*) My, oh my, my cupboards are bare.
We've only some soup and none to spare.
I wish I could work. I wish I could find
A job that could use my intelligent mind.

Please tell me, oh, please, why this life is so hard?
Oh, why is it me who was dealt a bad card?
My husband is dead, my house is for sale.
I've nothing to lose, but I'm certain to fail.

I can't go on living this terrible life.
And why should my son put up with such strife?
How long, how long must this misery last?
I wish I were dead or could disappear fast.

Jack: (*enters*) Mother, oh mother, I'm ready for school.
I'm making straight A's; I'm nobody's fool.
My best class is business, so you can sure trust
That soon we'll be leaving this life in the dust.

Mother: Jack, my dear son, don't you worry your head.
We'll make it somehow, or die in our bed.
I can't make more promises, for surely they'll bend;
But I do know someday that all this will end.

Now here, my dear, you take all this money
And buy us a goose that doesn't look funny.
On your way home from

school, just stop by the store
And tell Mr. Merchant who the big goose is for.

Now don't lose this money; it's all that we've got.
I'm counting on you to buy us a lot.
So shop very careful 'cause when spent, it's all gone.
Next time we need money, we may just have to pawn.

Jack: Like I said, Mother dear, I'm a good businessman.
You can count on me to make my demands.
"A goose, Mr. Merchant, the best in your shop.
It's for my sweet mother."
And then watch him hop.

Mother: Oh, Jack, you're so hopeful; you make life less tart.
You're the light of my eyes and a song in my heart.
Now hurry along, and don't be too late.
Remember, tonight we've a goose for a date.

(*Dim lights as* **Mother** *sits down. Then bring up lights, indicating that it's later in the day.*)

Jack: Mother, where are you? Come and see what I bought.
I got a great deal on this vine in a pot.
He said it would bring us true food and some drink.
Just believe with our hearts; it does more then we think.

Mother: That money was all that we had in the world,
And you gave it away on some whimsical whirl.
What can we do with a silly old weed?
How can it supply us with all that we need?
Throw it away! Get it out of my sight.
Then go to your room and turn out the light.
That goose was our meal and our one last big fight.
But look what you've done – brought darkness not light.

(**Jack** *sadly walks away. Lights move away from chairs and* **Mother** *and focus on* **Jack**.)

Jack: Will she ever understand that there's hope in this vine
To take us from here to a

new life divine?
We may not have anything
left to our name,
But the man said this vine
was not just a big game.

He said he's the gardener
of this unique vine,
And if I believed, a full life
would be mine.
Oh, please, Mr. Gardener,
don't end up a fake.
I gave all I had, and I've
got much at stake.

My mother is angry. My
friends turned away.
Things used to be rough,
but not like today.
They think I'm a fool for
having some hope,
But I've got to believe
there's a solution to cope.

I'm staying right here and
wait 'til it grows.
I know it will grow right in
front of my nose.
I believe Mr. Gardener was
telling it straight.
The world may be laugh-
ing, but the vine is my fate.

(**Jack** *falls asleep, the lights go out.*
Vine grows. Lights come on.)

Jack: Jiminy crickets, gosh, gee,
holy cow!
Look at the vine, World.
Tell me who's laughing
now?
I knew it would happen. I
knew it'd come true;
Or my name isn't Jack, and
the sky isn't blue.

(*pretends to climb*)

I'm gonna climb this big
vine all the way to the top,
And no one can stop me –
not even a cop.
I hope friends and family
will some day forgive
My insisting there must be
a better way to live.

(**Jack** *gets to the top and looks over.*
Lights come up on the banquet table.
Elegantly dressed people *are sitting at*
the table and talking. **Giant** *stands with*
hands on his hips and speaks.)

Giant: (*boldly*) Fee, Fi, Fo, Fum.
Welcome my boy, you
have finally come.
Bring on the music, the
dancing, the food.
Our guest of honor is here,
one very cool dude.

His own mother's love, his

friends, and his meal,
were his sacrifice to get this
incredible deal.
So come one, come all,
let's give him his prize,
For his faith and his hope
still shine in his eyes.

Come here, my son Jack.
Get off of your knees.
Partake of this banquet. Sit
here next to me.
My pleasure increases in
this land of great giving
As you now receive the
eternal joy in living.

Jack: Oh, thank you, kind sir.
Please tell me why
I am able to be here with
you in the sky?
My faith in the vine seems
too simple to be
The reason that all this is
given to me.

Giant: Jack, you're a boy who
gives me much pleasure,

And it's with great pride
that I love you without
measure.
The vine is the way for the
hope that's in you
To give all you had. This we
all have to do.

This is just the beginning of
your life here above.
It's from me to you, with all
of my love.

(**All** *raise their glasses to* **Jack**. *Lights out.*)

Discussion Questions
1. How would you define faith?
2. What steps of faith have you ever taken?
3. On a scale of 1-10, where does your faith lie? Why?
4. Read Proverbs 3:5-6. Why is it so hard to trust in God?
5. What in your life do you struggle to let go of and trust God?

THE FULL LIFE

Debra J. Poling

Characters

Ann   average high-school student

Peg   soap opera maniac, high-school student

Diane   sorority-type, high-school student

Tad   overbearing, cocky, lover-boy-type high-school student.

Burt   gullible, air-headed high-school student.

Stage is empty, except for a table. Each person enters carrying a representation of what they're into, but the audience doesn't necessarily see the objects until they are given to Ann.

Ann: (*enters carrying a box*) Hi. I'm Ann. And this is my life. (*holds up box, then sets it on the table*) You see, I know that there are only so many hours in a day, and I have to choose carefully what I get involved with. First, there's my family (*holds up portrait*). I try to make sure I spend time with them. I figure I owe them the pleasure of my presence regularly. Besides, I kind of like them. (*returning portrait to box*) Next is school (*holds up books*). I plan so I can attend all my classes as well as complete my homework. I'm going to college, so I need to take school seriously. (*returns books to box*) Which leads me to the next aspect of my life — my job (*holds up a fast-food uniform*). It's not very good pay, but it will help with college expenses. (*returns uniform to box*) And finally, and probably most importantly, is my relationship with God (*holds up a Bible*). By keeping close to him, I receive his guidance in all the other aspects of my life. (*returning Bible to box*) So here's my life, full, but not unmanageable.

Peg: (*enters with **Diane**, talking about the latest soap opera news*) I can't believe you missed what happened with Jenny and Greg's marriage. And I'm just positive that Liza is pregnant from that guy who raped her. But it's a relief now that Jesse and Angie have their baby back, don't you think?

Diane: It sure is. (*noticing* **Ann**) Oh, hi, Ann.

Ann: Hi, Diane. Hi, Peg. What'cha talking about?

Peg: You didn't see it either? Why *All My Children,* of course.

Diane: It was a real hot one today.

Ann: Oh. (*sheepishly*) I don't watch the soaps.

Peg: (*absolutely aghast*) You don't watch the soaps?

Ann: Ah … no.

Peg: What? Do you live in a cave? Everyone watches *All My Children.*

Ann: I guess I just don't have the time.

Peg: Time? What time? It's only one measly hour a day. You could fit it in.

Ann: I don't know. (*tilting her box so* **Peg** *can see how full it is*)

My life is pretty full.

Peg: (*holding up a box of detergent*) *All My Children* would fit in here if you just shuffle things around. (*squeezes detergent box into Ann's box*) See?

Ann: (*pleasantly surprised*) Oh, I guess I can fit more in my life than I thought.

Diane: I'm glad to hear you say that. We'll see you on Friday night then, right?

Ann: What's Friday night?

Diane: Peg, I knew she'd forget. Ann, it's our monthly FSS meeting.

Ann: FSS?

Diane: Future Sorority Sisters. This is your last chance to be accepted.

Ann: Diane, I know it would be great to be with you, but I just don't have the time.

Diane: We'll see about that. (*looks in Ann's box and holds up the books*) What are these in here for?

Ann: That's my homework.

Diane: So much? Nobody does this much homework.

Ann: Well, I want to get into college.

Diane: So do all the FSS'ers. But you don't see us doing all our homework. (*handing first one book and then the other to* **Peg**) Let's just get rid of Spanish and Calculus, (*showing an FSS poster and then placing in Ann's box*) then FSS will fit in nicely, and you can still spend a little time on homework.

Ann: Well, I guess I can cut back a bit on the homework. And I really want to be with the future Sorority Sisters.

Diane: Great. Then we'll see you Friday. (**Peg** *and* **Diane** *exit with Ann's books.*)

Ann: Yeah, see ya Friday. (*looking in box*). Well, things are a bit shuffled around, but look what great things I added to my life – soaps and sororities.

Tad: (*enters singing a love song*) Annie, baby, there you are. I've been looking all over for you.

Ann: (*moonstruck*) You have?

Tad: Yeah. I just couldn't wait to be with you.

Ann: You couldn't?

Tad: You know how I feel about … my woman!

Ann: (*coming to her senses a bit*) Yeah. Ah … you know I'm glad you like me, Tad, but I just don't want to get too involved right now.

Tad: Oh, Baby, I just can't live without you.

Ann: I just don't have time for a serious relationship.

Tad: Time? Why you can fit me in right here (*takes family portrait from box and puts in a big red heart*). See? A perfect fit.

Ann: But what about my family?

Tad: Honey, we'll make our own family.

Ann: *Now?*

Tad: No, Baby ... when we're married.

Ann: (*starry-eyed again*) Well, I have spent a lot of time with my family.

Tad: With me around, you'll never miss them.

Ann: Oh, Tad!

Tad: Oh, Baby. I'll pick you up at seven-thirty tonight. 'Til then, my sweet. (*exits, taking portrait with him*)

Ann: 'Til then ... (*remembering what **Tad** said*) ... we'll make our own family ... (*big sigh*).

Burt: (*enters very excitedly*) Ann, Ann, have I got some great news for you!

Ann: What? Oh, Burt. What did you say?

Burt: I said, this is your lucky day. (*handing her a newspaper*) Here, read this.

Ann: What? Where?

Burt: Right there.

Ann: "Virgos are in for a special life-changing offer this week. Be open to new suggestions and schedule changes." This is amazing. This is exactly what has been happening to me just this afternoon.

Burt: And people say this is just co-incidence. I think you should follow your horoscope more closely.

Ann: Ah, I don't think so. I believe in God, and somehow this stuff doesn't go along with his Word.

Burt: The *Bible*?! Come on, Ann. Get with the times. Everyone reads their horoscopes. Why do you think every newspaper prints it every day?

Ann: Well, I don't have the time.

Burt: Ann, all you have to do is re-arrange things a little (*digs in her box*) and get rid of some things (*takes out her Bible*) and then everything will fit fine, horoscope and all.

Ann: Burt, I don't think I ...

Burt: Now don't put up an argument. Believe me, this will be life-changing. See ya around, you lucky little Virgo you! (*exits taking her Bible with him*)

Ann: (*awestruck, looking at her box in amazement. After a moment notices audience again.*) Ah … hi, I'm Ann. (*despairingly*) And this is my life. (*getting control of herself*) You see, I know that there's only so many hours in a day, and I have to choose carefully what I get involved with. First, there's the Soaps, next is the FSS'ers, and then there's Tad, and finally (*sounding lost*) my relationship with my horoscope. Yep, here's my life – (*sadly*) full, but not unman-ageable. (*turns to examine the contents of her box*)

Discussion Questions

1. How do you respond when people suggest ways you should spend your time? Explain why you answer as you do.
2. Why do people let their lives get too full? Is your life too full for any of those reasons? Explain.
3. Do you remember a time in your life when you felt like you were doing too many unimportant things? What was that like? How did you get into that predicament? How did you get out?
4. What things seem to creep in and rob you of your time with God? What can you do to keep that from happening?

CHAPTER SIX

Peer and Family Relations

YOU ARE MY HERO

Debra J. Poling

Characters

Burt Harris star receiver for high school football team, having a bad game

Melvin Murdock water boy for the team, friend and admirer of Burt

Announcer offstage adult announcer of game

Coach Philips stereotypical football coach

Cheerleader(s) use one or several cheerleaders

Other player(s) use one or several football players

The song "Wind Beneath My Wings" sung by Bette Midler may be used at the end of this sketch.

Other players *are warming the bench at the last football game of*

the season. The Falcons are behind, largely due to Harris's blunders. **Melvin** *is standing near the bench cheering the team on.* **One or several cheerleaders** *are cheering.* **Coach Philips** *is pacing angrily.*

Announcer: And that's the end of the third quarter. The Falcons are behind by seven.

Cheerleader: That's all right, that's okay, we're gonna beat 'em anyway. Yea, Falcons! (**Harris** *enters*)

Melvin: Way to go, Burt. You left his jock behind!

Harris: (*depressed at self*) Ah, knock it off, Melvin.

Melvin: Here, have some water.

Harris: (*very down*) Thanks. I don't know what's wrong with me today.

Melvin: Burt, you're just having a bad ...

Philips: (*enters and crosses to* **Harris**) Harris, I don't want excuses ... I want action. What's happening to you out there?

Harris: Coach, I don't ...

Philips: Jones is hitting you right in the numbers, and you've dropped it all day.

Harris: I can't seem to ...

Philips: You're not looking the ball into your hands. You've dropped three in a row.

Melvin: Coach, I know he can do ...

Philips: Murdock, shut up!

Melvin: But sir, I ...

Philips: Murdock!

Harris: That's okay, Mel, he's right. I just can't seem to concentrate.

Cheerleader: We've got the ball, now they're gonna fall. Yea, Falcons!

Philips: (*to* **cheerleader**) Get

out of here!

(**Cheerleader** *is offended and goes to the other side of the stage.*)

Melvin: Coach, don't knock Burt down. He'll do it.

Philips: (*holding* **Harris'** *face right at his*) How much do you pay this guy to stand up for you, ya wimp? Now you listen to me, and you listen to me good. You've got one more chance, then I'm taking you out of the game. You either hang on to the thing or hang it up. Ya got it?

Harris: (*softly and sadly*) Yes, Coach.

Philips: I can't hear you.

Harris: (*louder*) Yes, Coach.

Philips: WHAT?!

Harris: YES, COACH! (**Coach** *goes to other side of stage and talks to the* **other player(s)** *who have left the bench*

also.) Mel, I can't go out there. I just don't have it.

Melvin: Don't have it? What are you talking about? You've got the best record of any player in the conference.

Harris: *Did* have. My hands are like bricks today.

Melvin: Burt, you've got the hands, you just gotta look it in. Ya know, just look it in.

Harris: Mel, I always thought I was a cut above the others. I've dreamed about someday play-ing pro ball. Who was I trying to kid?

Melvin: (*getting a bit angry at Burt's self-pity*) Burt, on every single play you had your man beat. This last play you had Bowers decked out.

Harris: Hey, I see what you're trying to do, but it's no good. (*staring at his* *hands, then holding them up*) They're hard ... like bricks!

Melvin: (*getting angrier*) You know something, Harris, maybe you're right. Maybe you're not made of tough enough stuff. A couple of bad plays and you're beating yourself. If you want the pros, you gotta have the stuff pros are made of — you gotta push yourself, meet the challenge. But you just dig a hole of self-pity and crawl in. I had you figured all wrong.

Harris: Mel ... I didn't ...

Melvin: Ah, shut up! (*turns his back on* **Harris**.

Harris (*reflecting for a moment, looks at his hands, then speaks with determination*) They're soft ...

Melvin: (*still with his back to* **Harris**) And you can

bring it in. Just gotta concentrate.

Philips: All right men, get out there. (*to* **Harris**) And get it right!

(**Harris** and **the other player(s)** *leave the stage. The* **cheerleader(s)** *starts cheering.* **Mel** *stands up and cheers Harris on.*)

Announcer: And we're back in the game. Here they come out of the huddle. They're setting up single-back. They're sending wide receivers left. Here's the count ... the snap ... Montana drops back, looks for a receiver ... he can't find one open ... he steps up into the pocket ... he's going for broke ... he throws to Harris. He has a step on his man. He's going to it. He's got it! A touchdown! The crowd is going wild. The score is tied. What a play for the Falcons.

(**Harris** and **others** *enter.* **All** *are cheering and jumping on everyone.*)

Philips: I don't know what's got into you, but whatever it is, keep it there!

(**Mel** *is standing on the side, away from the others.* **Harris** *sees him and begins to walk toward him.*)

All right men, let's get that point!

(**The other player(s)** *runs out.* **Coach** *and* **cheerleader** *are on far side of stage.* **Harris** *comes to* **Melvin**, *who is by the bench.*)

Melvin: I knew you could do it! I just knew you could!

Harris: Yeah, you did, didn't you?

Melvin: (*shyly*) Well … you are a cut above.

Harris: You know what, Mel … you are a cut above. (*grabs* **Mel's** *head under arm in headlock and "punches" with the other arm.*)

(*Close the sketch with the song "Wind Beneath My Wings"*)

Discussion Questions

1. How much influence do your friends have on your abilities? How does that influence show?
2. When is the last time you really had doubts about whether you could do a hard task or job? What did that feel like?
3. When has someone's encouragement meant a lot to you? What was it like?
4. Why do you think people seem to do much better at something when someone believes in them?
5. How could you help someone who was discouraged? Discuss how Romans 15:1, 2 and 5 can guide you.

THE DECEPTION OF DIANE

Sharon Sherbondy

Characters
Sarah average teenager
Carrie sensitive, caring seventeen year old
Diane self-absorbed, slightly spoiled teenager
Margo average teenager
Janice average teenager

Stage is set and decorated like a dorm room at a boarding school, with a desk, banners, books, and a few chairs. Carrie is sitting at the desk studying. Sarah enters, crying.

Sarah: Carrie?

Carrie: Sarah, what's wrong?

Sarah: I'm sorry to bother you, but do you have a minute?

Carrie: Sure. Come on in.

Sarah: (*looks around*) Is *she* here?

Carrie: No, she's downstairs getting some pop.

Sarah: I'll make it quick, then.

Carrie: Come on, sit down. What's wrong?

Sarah: I just got my calculus midterm back. I flunked.

Carrie: Oh, Sarah. I'm so sorry.

Sarah: What am I going to tell my folks? They'll be furious.

Diane: (*enters carrying a can of pop*) So, anyway, Carrie, where was I? Oh, I remember. I was just ... Oh, Sarah, hi. You're just in time to hear about when my dad took me to meet Kirk Cameron.

Sarah: I've got to get going.

Diane: But you've got to hear this.

Carrie: Uh, Diane ...

Diane: He was such a hunk. What a hunk. He was gorgeous, and of course we hit it off right away. He said he thought I was cute and interesting, which didn't surprise me because, well, I've heard that from people all my life. When I was a little girl, it was always, "Oh, Diane, you're so cute, you're so talented." I play most instruments, you know. I guess I was what you'd call a gifted child. That's why I'm here – because of the music program. It's expensive, I know, but my family is pretty wealthy. But then I suppose you could tell that just by looking at me.

I used to try and hide the fact that my family had money, but people could see right through me, so I just resigned myself to being happy and rich. I try to exercise at least five times a week, you know. I've come up with some great routines. They're all original. Here, let me show you some. I just love it when I'm creative, which is most of the time, I might add. (**Diane** continues to talk and show exercises.)

Sarah: What is she doing?

Carrie: She's showing us her aerobic routine.

Sarah: I've gotta go before I get sick. (turns to leave)

Diane: (stops her routine) Hey, what's the matter?

(**Sarah** pauses, putting her head in her hand.)

Carrie: Sarah's upset because she just found out she flunked her calc midterm.

Diane: Oh, no kidding. Did I tell you that I had my colors done last night?

Sarah: (looks at **Diane** in amazement) What?

Diane: My colors. You know, I went to a makeup party, and they told me I'm a Summer, the cool season.

Carrie: Diane, what does this have to do with Sarah flunking calc?

Diane: Carrie, I just spent $800 last week buying all the wrong colors for me. So I can really identify with how you're feeling, Sarah. It was devastating. I cried my eyes out. And now what am I going to do with all those new clothes? I suppose I could give them to you guys. You don't usually care how you look.

Sarah: Bye, Carrie.

Diane: Hey, Sarah, glad I could help. (*knocks over can of pop*) Oops. Oh, knocked over my pop. (*kneels behind bed to clean it up*)

Carrie: Hope you get to feeling better. We can talk more later.

Sarah: Yeah, in the meantime I'm going to put a contract out on her.

Carrie: Now, Sarah, she means well. I'll come to your room later.

Sarah: Okay. See you. (*exits*)

(**Janice** *and* **Margo** *enter*)

Janice: Hey, Carrie, we're just going out for something to eat. Want to come along?

Carrie: Uh, yeah. Let me ask Diane.

Margo: No, don't ask Diane! Come on, Carrie, we want to have an enjoyable meal.

Janice: Yeah, really. Every time that blabbermouth shows up, I lose my appetite and get sick to my stomach.

Carrie: (*embarrassed*) You guys.

Janice: Come on, Carrie. Nobody likes her.

Margo: Yeah, she's a disease that everyone avoids.

Carrie: (*nervous*) Listen, I'd really like to go with you guys, but I have a lot of studying to do. Maybe another time.

Margo: Okay. See ya. (*exits*)

Janice: Maybe tomorrow. (*exits*)

(**Carrie** *stands there feeling very awkward and embarrassed.* **Diane** *stands up looking very hurt.*)

Carrie: (*smiling*) Well, did you get that pop all cleaned up?

Diane: Is it true – what they said?

Carrie: Come on, Diane. Don't pay any attention to them.

Diane: Answer my question. Is it true?

Carrie: Well, Diane, that's hard to say.

Diane: Carrie, come on! Tell me! Is it true that nobody likes me – that I'm a "disease that everyone avoids?"

Carrie: (*pause*) Yes. It's true.

Diane: Why didn't you ever tell me?

Carrie: I thought you knew.

Diane: Carrie, how could I know unless someone told me?

Carrie: You couldn't tell by the way people act toward you? I mean, it seems obvious.

Diane: I feel like such a jerk.

Carrie: Diane, I'm sorry.

Diane: *You're* sorry? You're not the one making people feel sick to their stomachs. I just can't believe you never said anything to me.

Carrie: I didn't want to hurt your feelings.

Diane: How do you think I feel now?! Carrie, I thought we were best friends.

Carrie: We *are* best friends.

Diane: Then you should have said something!

Carrie: Diane, what would you have wanted me to do? Just walk right up to your face and say, "Uh, listen, Diane, I'm tired of hearing you talk nonstop all day long, especially about yourself. So could you do me and the world a favor and shut up?"

Diane: Better to my face than behind my back.

Carrie: You would have been furious with me.

Diane: So?

Carrie: So, that's why I never said anything.

Diane: Because I would have gotten mad at you? I can't believe this! You would rather I look like a jerk for the rest of my life than put up with one day of my being mad at you? How selfish can you get?!

Carrie: I never thought about it like that before. (*pause*) I guess if you can't count on your best friend to be honest with you, who can you count on?

Diane: I'm so embarrassed. How can I face all those people again?

Carrie: Maybe if you could just try talking a little less.

Diane: To think that all this time I've been working so hard to feel like I belong, to make people like me. I can't tell you how often I used to dream about going away to college and making new friends, not that I want to replace you or any-thing …

Carrie: Uh, Diane …

Diane: But, you know, just to be in all the clubs and to date the star quarterback and to be, maybe, homecoming queen …

Carrie: Diane! (*puts tape over Di-ane's mouth*) You're absolutely right. I should have taped your mouth shut years ago. And so from now on I'm going to be honest with you.

You got it?!

Diane: (*humbly nods her head*)

Carrie: Now, I'm going to go see if the girls have left yet. (*yells out the door*) Hey, Janice, you guys still around? Come here for a second.

Diane: (*pulls tape off*) What are you doing?

Carrie: (*smiling*) I'm going to give you a chance to purchase some friendships.

Diane: Huh?

(**Janice, Margo,** *and* **Sarah** *enter*)

Carrie: Girls, Diane is going to take us all out for pizza.

(**The Three Girls** *look slightly disgusted.*)

Diane: Carrie, what are you doing? I'm not going to pay for ev-erybody's meal, not that I couldn't, I mean. Money's no object or anything, but I was, you know, going to buy a new wardrobe because like I already told you I got my col-ors done last night and I was thinking that maybe it might be a good idea if ...

Carrie: *DIANE!* (**Diane** *puts the tape back over her mouth*) Girls, meet the new Diane Templeton.

Sarah: Free pizza, Diane with a taped mouth; this day may not turn out to be a total disaster after all.

Janice: That looks good on you, Diane. It's definitely your color.

Discussion Questions

1. Have you ever confronted or thought about confronting a friend whose behavior was unacceptable? What did you say or want to say? What stopped you?
2. Is it a sin to hurt someone's feelings? Why or why not?
3. For what areas in your life would you like your friends to hold you accountable?
4. Matthew 18:15 says to confront in private (not gossip). What's the harm in a little gossip?
5. What does gossip do for a person?

MY LIPS ARE SEALED

Debra J. Poling

Characters
Kelly ⎫
Pam ⎪
Peter ⎬ all high-school students
Chuck ⎪
Ann ⎭

Kelly *and* **Pam** *are standing and talking in the hallway of a high school.* **Pam** *is holding a newspaper;* **Kelly** *is carrying a few books and papers. Each character enters from stage left and exits stage right.*

Kelly: Ah, only one more hour of school, then time to go home.

Pam: I hope you have big plans for this weekend.

Kelly: Why's that?

Pam: Here, let me read your horoscope for tomorrow. "Be on the alert for a sexy Sagittarius. Something terribly wonderful is about to happen."

Kelly: I can tell you the terribly wonderful happening for this weekend – I have to baby-sit Kyle. Mom and Dad are going to Indiana for a wedding this weekend.

Pam: Sounds more like "wonderfully terrible"!

Kelly: And as far as a "sexy Sagittarius," guess who is one?

Pam: Kyle?

Kelly: Sagittarius, yes; sexy, impossible. No ten year old is sexy, especially when he's your brother!

Pam: (*throwing the paper on the floor*) Well, I never believe these things anyway.

Kelly: You know, Pam, sometimes I hate being a big sister.

Pam: Well, at least you have a brother. Let me tell you, it's no fun being an only child.

Kelly: For just one week I'd like to

know what it's like to be the only kid in our family. (*unknowingly drops a letter as she looks at her watch.* **Pam** *doesn't see it either.*) Oh, I gotta go. Time for algebra.

Pam: Okay, Kelly, I guess I'll see you on Monday, then.

Kelly: Yeah. Bye, Pam.

(**Kelly** *exits.* **Pam** *watches her leave and continues staring in that direction.* **Peter** *enters.*)

Peter: Hey, Pam, what'cha thinking about?

Pam: Huh? Oh, I was just thinking about Kelly.

Peter: I know what you mean. I like to think about Kelly, too!

Pam: No. I mean I'm worried about her.

Peter: Why's that?

Pam: Well, don't spread this around, but she just told me that she really hates her brother.

Peter: You mean Kyle?

Pam: Yeah. I've seen anger in people like that before on TV and they usually end up doing something rash.

Peter: Ah, come on, Pam. I've seen Kelly and Kyle together. She really likes him.

Pam: Now don't tell anybody, but she just told me she wonders what it would be like to be an only child!

Peter: That's silly. The only way she could become an only child is to … (*halts abruptly, realizing what Pam is getting at*).

Pam: Shhh! I gotta go. Don't tell anyone about this, okay?

Peter: My lips are sealed.

(**Pam** *exits.* **Peter** *watches her leave and contines staring in that direction.* **Chuck** *enters.*)

Chuck: Hey Peter! What'cha thinking about?

Peter: Huh? Oh, I was just thinking about Pam.

Chuck: I know what you mean. I like to think about Pam, too!

Peter: No, I mean I was thinking about Kelly.

Chuck: Hey, I like to think about Kelly, too!

Peter: No, no! I was thinking about what Pam just told me about Kelly.

Chuck: What was that?

Peter: Well, I'm not supposed to tell anyone.

Chuck: Hey, who's anyone? I'm Chuck, ol' boy. You know, your good friend Chuck – the one you tell everything to.

Peter: All right. Just keep this to yourself.

Chuck: My lips are sealed.

Peter: Pam just told me that Kelly is so mad at her little brother that she's threatening to kill him.

Chuck: Come on. That sounds like a story Pam would invent.

Peter: I know it sounds crazy. But I'm really worried for Kyle's sake. I've heard that Kelly has a real hot temper. And you know her dad has that woodworking shop in his garage. It would be easy for her to do something awful to Kyle in a fit of anger.

Chuck: Stop it, Pete! You're spooking me.

Peter: I shouldn't have told you.

Chuck: Naw, that's all right.

Peter: Look, I gotta go to class. I'll pick you up tonight at seven o'clock sharp.

Chuck: Okay. See you then.

(**Chuck** *watches* **Pete** *leave and stares in that direction.* **Ann** *enters.*)

Ann: Hey, Chuck, what'cha thinking about?

Chuck: Huh? Oh, I was just thinking about Peter.

Ann: I know what you mean. I like to think about Peter, too.

Chuck: No, I mean I was thinking about what Peter told me about what Pam told him about Kelly.

Ann: (*confused*) Huh?

Chuck: Ah, never mind. I'm sworn to secrecy, anyway.

Ann: Is there something wrong with Pam?

Chuck: No, Pam's fine.

Ann: Ah ha! So there's something wrong with Kelly.

Chuck: How did you know?

Ann: Word travels quick, I guess.

Chuck: What did you hear?

Ann: Hey, you can't fool me with that old trick. You tell me what you know first, then I'll tell you if it's what I heard.

Chuck: Okay. Oh, Ann, this is terrible.

Ann: What happened?

Chuck: I thought you knew.

Ann: I do ... I mean, I know ... it's just awful.

Chuck: I bet Kelly will get twenty-five years in jail for this.

Ann: Jail?

Chuck: Yeah, you don't chain-saw your little brother into pieces, bury him in the backyard, and get off with parole.

Ann: Chain-saw her brother?

Chuck: Yeah, I thought you knew.

Ann: No! I didn't know that!

Chuck: Oh, Ann. Kelly seemed like such a nice girl. Listen, I gotta go. Oh, this is awful.

(**Chuck** *exits.* **Ann** *watches him go.* **Kelly** *enters.*)

Kelly: Ah, there it is. (*picks up her letter*).

Ann: (*screams*) What are you doing here?

Kelly: I'm just picking up a letter I dropped here earlier.

Ann: (*totally ignoring what she said and still in shock*). How could you do such a thing? How could you?

Kelly: (*very confused by Ann's re-*

action.) I didn't mean to. It just slipped out.

Ann: That's terrible, just terrible. (*runs out, screaming*)

Kelly: (*in utter amazement, watches* **Ann**, *then shrugs her shoulders and says jokingly*) Boy, if she gets so upset about littering, I wonder how she'd react if I really did something awful … like kill my brother!

Discussion Questions

1. When have you heard about or even passed on a story about someone that wasn't completely accurate? How did you feel when the whole truth came out? What effects did the incident have on the person the misinformation was about?

2. What's the difference between spreading a rumor and telling accurately a terrifically juicy, all-true story about someone? Is it ever right to share information that puts someone in a bad light?

3. The Bible says the tongue "sets the whole course of (a person's) life on fire" (James 3:6). Why do you think fire is used to describe what a person's speech can do?

4. What's wrong with "I wasn't supposed to tell anyone, but if you promise not to tell, I'll tell you" kinds of discussions? Do your friends ever tell you secrets that they really want you to spread around? What do you think about that way of getting the word out?

5. Read Proverbs 11:9-13. Pick out a phrase or verse and explain why you're glad God included it in the Bible. Why would the world be better off if it were obeyed?

FAMILY THERAPLAY

Sharon Sherbondy

Characters

Doctor middle-aged male or female, dressed in suit
Fred middle-aged father
Millicent middle-aged mother
Greg average teenager
Father middle-aged Nazi guard/caring parent
Mother middle-aged Nazi guard/caring parent
Son compliant/rebellious teenager

This sketch requires two sets of actors playing the same characters. Stage-right actors remain unaware of stage-left actors. Stage right is set with a desk, telephone, four chairs facing desk. Stage left is set as a living room. **Son** *is seated in one of the chairs in the living room, reading a magazine. Stage left remains in black. Lights come up on stage right.* **Doctor, Fred, Millicent,** *and* **Greg** *are standing near the desk.*

Doctor: (*shaking hands with the family*) Hello, I'm Dr. Haines.

Fred: Hello, I'm Fred Jones, and this is my wife, Millicent.

Milly: Hello, Dr. Haines. We appreciate so much your seeing us.

Doctor: That's what I'm here for. And this must be Greg. (*extends hand to* **Greg**, *who doesn't respond*) Well, why don't we sit down over here and make ourselves comfortable.

Milly: Thank you.

Doctor: Well, now, who would like to begin and tell me what's happening with the Joneses?

Fred: Well, Doctor, we just can't seem to get anywhere with Greg. He doesn't do what we say; he doesn't listen to us. He just fights us every step of the way.

Milly: We're at our wit's end. We love Greg and want the best for him, but he won't accept our love.

Greg: (*under his breath*) Love. Right.

Doctor: Greg, did you want to say something? Or do you agree with everything your parents have said?

Greg: Are you kidding? You're only hearing their side of the story. And if you ask me, it's pretty warped.

Doctor: Then why don't you fill me in on how you see things?

Greg: What for? You're on their side.

Doctor: Well, you're not leaving me much choice. All I've go to go on is what they've told me.

Greg: All right, then, I'll tell you what it's really like. I'll give you all the gory details if you want.

Doctor: Whatever you want to tell me.

Greg: Okay, okay. Here's a typical Saturday morning.

(*Lights fade on stage right. Lights up on stage left.*)

I'm sitting in the living room minding my own business when in march Mr. and Mrs. Adolph Hitler.

(*Enter **Mother** and **Father** wearing Nazi clothes with arm bands and mustaches. **Son** is cowering.*)

Well, before I can say anything, they start interrogating me about what time I got in the night before.

Father: (*with German accent*) You vill tell us vhat time you got in last night or you vill pay ze consequences.

Mother: (*with German accent*) Come on, out viz it. (*breathing heavily*) Although nossing vould gife me more pleasure zan to *make* you talk.

Greg: So I tell them as nicely as I can.

Son: (*quivering*) Good morning, Father. Good morning, Mother. I got in last night at the time you told me to get in.

Greg: But they don't believe me. They never do.

Mother: You lie. You lie, I tell you.

Greg: So what do they do? They start beating me.

Father: (*grabbing son*) You did *not* get in at ten-thirty. It vas my night for guard duty, so I know you did not get in zen. (*begins slapping him*) You vill not lie to me anymore. You vill come out viz de truth.

Mother: Here, let me at him for a vile. (*slapping son*) Vhat time, liar? Vhat time vas it?

Greg: Okay, so I finally tell them.

Son: All right, all right. I'll tell you. Just please don't hurt me anymore. It was ten-thirty-five. I was five minutes late. (*begins sobbing*)

Greg: I'm telling you, my parents are super strict. What's a few minutes? At least I came home. Well, need I tell you what happened next? They tied me up for who knows how long, getting their kicks out of it.

(**Mother** *and* **Father** *are tying up* **Son**.)

Son: Please, anything but this. Please!

Father: Ha! You are lucky ve don't do vorse tings to you.

Mother: Ve are fery creatife, your father and I. Lie again to us and you vill see vhat ve can do.

Father: You vill stay in here until ve are ready to deal vit you again.

Mother: Two or tree years, perhaps. Who knows? (**Mother** *and* **Father** *laugh.*)

Greg: Well, as far as I was concerned, they might as well have just taken a gun and shot me.

(**Son** *looks horror-stricken at* **Greg**, *frantically shaking his head.* **Mother** *and* **Father** *look at each other in delighted surprise, smile at the audience, then* **Father** *reaches into his inside pocket and pulls out a gun.* **Father** *aims the gun at* **Son's** *head.* **Greg** *continues unaware of stage left.*)

Of course, that's just a figure of speech. You know what I mean.

(**Son** *falls back in his chair in relief.* **Mother** *and* **Father** *show their disappointment. Lights fade on stage left.*)

Doctor: My, Greg, that's quite a story.

Greg: You don't believe me, do you? Well, it's true. All of it.

Doctor: Why don't we hear what your parents have to say?

Milly: Oh, Dr. Haines, nothing of what Greg said was true. We love him. All we want to do is teach him to behave.

Fred: She's right, Doctor. Here, let us tell you about a typical Saturday morning. We try to start out the day on a good note.

(*Light comes up on stage left.* **Son** *is wearing a black leather jacket and sunglasses and is sprawled across the chair.* **Mother** *and* **Father** *walk in.*)

Mother: Good morning, Son. Did you have a nice evening last night?

Son: None of your business.

Father: What'd you do?

Son: Hey, can't I have any privacy? Do I have to tell you everything?

Mother: Of course not. We're just interested in you.

Son: Yeah, well, butt out.

Fred: So, when things start going downhill, I figure now is as good a time as any to bring up the problem at hand.

Father: Son, I think we need to talk again about your curfew.

Mother: We know you got in late last night.

Son: It's too bad that you two don't have lives of your own to live instead of having to run mine.

Milly: You see, we don't like to come right out and accuse Greg, so we give him the opportunity to be honest with us.

Father: Son, what time did you get in last night?

Son: Didn't you have your guard dogs out as usual?

Fred: Greg enjoys pushing us so that we have no choice but to become stern.

Father: All right, Son, that remark was unnecessary. We know that you didn't get in at ten-thirty.

Son: Ten-thirty, twelve o'clock, what's the difference? Hey, count yourselves lucky that I came home at all.

Milly: Doctor, maybe we're wrong, but we've found that the only way to reach Greg or to teach him anything is to get him where it hurts.

Mother: You know how we hate to resort to punishing you.

Son: So don't.

Father: Son, you're grounded for two weeks.

Son: Two weeks?! Are you nuts?!

Father: You've got to learn to do what you're told – no matter how old you are.

Son: Do me a favor – just shoot me and end my life now. I'd be a lot better off.

Doctor: So what happened next, Mr. Jones?

Fred: That's basically it.

Father: The discussion is now closed. Two weeks and that is final.

Doctor: Well, this has been very interesting, but I think we should stop here and talk about what's just happened.

Greg: Really. I don't act like they described me.

Fred: And we're not Nazi soldiers.

Greg: Well, that's how you act.

Milly: And that's how you act!

Doctor: That's how you're picturing each other. I'm sure none of you is acting as bad as the other is describing.

Greg: Listen, anybody's who's as into punishment as they are …

Milly: Discipline, Dear, not punishment.

Doctor: Greg, we all get disciplined, either by our bosses or the government or our parents. We all need it now and then. It's a good thing – hard to take sometimes – but good.

I'm afraid our time is up for today. It looks like we've got our work cut out for us. Maybe next week we can talk about the kind of discipline that Greg would be open to.

Greg: Yeah. Like maybe Nintendo for only two hours instead of three each night.

Doctor: That's one possibility. See you next week?

Milly: Yes, Doctor. Thank you.

Fred: Yes, thank you.

Discussion Questions

1. What character would describe your parents? Why?
   (Hitler, Dr. Dobson, Mr. Rogers, Roseanne Barr)
2. How would your parents describe you? Why?
   (Prince, Madonna, Bart Simpson, Kirk Cameron, Tiffany)
3. What are some issues that you and your parents seem to battle over? Any ideas on resolving them?
4. What do you think the Bible means when it says, "Honor your father and your mother"?
5. How are you disciplined now? What are other options you might like to discuss with your parents?

PARENTING 101

Sharon Sherbondy

Characters
Mick   high-school junior
Sarah   high-school junior

Stage is set like a living room. **Sarah** *is sitting on a chair eating a cupcake.*

Mick: (*wearing pants and untucked shirt, carrying his shoes, yawning*) Oh, man. It's too early. What time did you get up?

Sarah: I've been up most of the night. That couch isn't the most comfortable thing to sleep on.

Mick: I've never had any trouble falling asleep on it.

Sarah: Well, then why didn't you sleep there and let me have the bed?

Mick: Because this is my house. Listen, we could have done this project at your house, remember?

Sarah: We would have if I'd known that I'd get stuck with this couch.

Mick: Don't start in again. We argued all last night. Let's just get through the day and be done with this assignment.

Sarah: I don't know why we even have to do this. I mean, how hard is it to be a parent, anyway? This Adult Preparation Class is a bit too much. They make parenting sound like Mission Impossible.

Mick: Hey, don't complain. This will be the easiest A we've ever gotten. (*pause*) What are you eating?

Sarah: A Hostess cupcake.

Mick: Aren't you gonna fix breakfast?

Sarah: (*stops in the middle of a chew and says with a mouth full of food*) No, are you?

Mick: You mean, that's your breakfast?

Sarah: Yeah. Something wrong with that?

Mick: Well, my mom usually fixes eggs, French toast, or at least cereal.

Sarah: Well, your "mommy's" not here.

Mick: According to the assignment, *you* are the mommy and *I* am the daddy. And the daddy is hungry.

Sarah: And this mommy doesn't fix breakfast. Besides, there isn't any.

Mick: What do you mean, there isn't any?

Sarah: Just what I said. There's no food in the house.

Mick: Well, why didn't you check before we went out last night? We could have stopped at the store.

Sarah: Because you were in such a stinking hurry to get to McDonald's and to the show, that's why. And what a stupid show it was, too.

Mick: *Bambi* isn't that bad.

Sarah: Maybe not, but your brother and sister were. They were loud and fidgety the whole time. I couldn't watch the show for having to watch them. What fun!

Mick: Speaking of Billy and Missy, where are they?

Sarah: In bed, I guess.

Mick: Shouldn't you be getting them up? We gotta get to school pretty soon.

Sarah: Can't you get them up? They're your brother and sister.

Mick: Yeah, but my …

Sarah: Don't tell me. Your mom does that, too. No wonder women age faster than men. They have to do everything.

Mick: Knock it off, will ya? All right, I'll go get them up. You find them something to eat.

Sarah: I told you, there isn't anything. The cupboards are bare, Mother Hubbard.

Mick: Well, isn't there a frozen pizza or something?

Sarah: For breakfast?!

Mick: Well, it beats Hostess cupcakes.

Sarah: Get serious, Mick.

Mick: Okay, okay. We'll go out for breakfast.

Sarah: We've got enough money to do that?

Mick: Sure.

Sarah: How much?

Mick: Enough.

Sarah: My, aren't we the private one!

Mick: Sarah, just hurry up and get ready. We gotta go.

Sarah: What do you mean, we gotta go? I haven't taken a shower yet. My hair's dirty. I don't have any makeup …

Mick: Yeah, I noticed.
Sarah: You're not exactly God's gift to women, you know.

Mick: Sarah, just shut up and get

ready. (*exits*)

Sarah: (*sits down and puts on her socks and shoes*) Okay, okay. Yes sir, yes sir. Where's my other shoe? I can't go to school like this! Well, come on. Let's get going.

Mick: (*enters*) All right.

Sarah: Where are the kids?

Mick: Getting dressed. I'll go out and start the car. Why don't you pick things up around here in the meantime?

Sarah: Me?! This is just as much your mess as it is mine.

Mick: You want to go out there and sit in a freezing car for ten minutes to get it started? Scrape the windows and …

Sarah: All right. I'll clean up.

Mick: Good. I'll be right back. (*exits*)

Sarah: (*starts picking things up*) This house is a mess. He is such a pig – oh, this is mine. Forget it. This is too much to clean up. (**Mick** *returns*) What's wrong?

Mick: The car's dead.

Sarah: Dead?! It won't do anything?

Mick: Nothing.

Sarah: Well, can't you fix it?

Mick: (*mocks her*) "Well, can't you fix it?" No, I can't fix it. My dad always takes care of the cars or takes them to get fixed.

Sarah: Okay. So call someone.

Mick: Do you know how much it costs for somebody to come and fix your car?

Sarah: You said you had some money, so let's use it.

Mick: Sarah, we don't have enough money to pay for the car to get fixed, to eat breakfast, to pay for the sitter, and to get gas.

Sarah: Gas?

Mick: (*sheepishly*) The car's out of gas, too.

Sarah: You're brilliant, you know that? If I had been in charge of the budget, we wouldn't be in this mess.

Mick: You're the one that wanted to go to the show.

Sarah: How was I to know the stupid car wouldn't run this morning?!

Mick: Ever try thinking?

(**Mick** and **Sarah** begin arguing. Doorbell rings.)

Mick: (*angrily*) I'll get it. (*exits*)

Sarah: I wish. (*sits down in chair*)

Mick: (*returns*) Did you call for the baby-sitter to come and pick up the kids?

Sarah: Yeah, is that her?

Mick: I can't believe it. You did something right.

Sarah: Don't start in again, Mick, because…

Mick: All right. We'll call a truce. We gotta get to school, anyway.

Sarah: I'm not going.

Mick: Why not?

Sarah: Because I didn't get any sleep last night, I'm hungry, I'm dirty, and I'm generally exhausted.

Mick: I guess it's not as easy as it looks. Should we call school and tell them or what?

Sarah: I don't know and I don't care.

Mick: Okay, so we'll just sit here.

Sarah: Fine with me. All I know is that if this is what it's like to be a parent, then I'd rather stay a teenager.

Discussion Questions

1. How is the work divided around your house?
2. How will the work be divided in your home if you get married?
3. How have your parents prepared you for living on your own?
4. What are you looking forward to when you move out of the house?
5. What are you not looking forward to when you move out?

OR ELSE

Sharon Sherbondy

Characters

Captain Davis	detective, Joe Friday-type
Sergeant	uniformed policeman
Ethel	nosy, busybody neighbor lady
Peterson	uniformed policeman
Ralph	middle-aged father
Judy	middle-aged mother
Tom	desperate teenager
Missy	little sister
Crowd (opt.)	variety of neighbor-types

At the scene of a crime. Flashing red lights. **Crowd** *gathered around, watching, whispering.* **Detective** *talking with the* **Sergeant***.*

Captain: Peterson, you go around the side of the house and see if you can get a glimpse of him through a window. Stay low. We don't want any trouble with him. (**Peterson** *exits*) Sergeant, have the parents gotten here yet?

Sergeant: No, sir. We're still trying to locate them. Neighbor says they're gone every Tuesday night, leaving the children alone.

Ethel: I knew something like this would happen, but no, no one listens to me. Well, all I can say is that it serves everyone right.

Captain: Sergeant, who is this woman?

Sergeant: She's the neighbor lady who's been filling us in on the family situation.

Ethel: I'll tell you anything you want to know. Of course, anything I say now is of little consequence.

Captain: True.

Ethel: Well, this whole mess could have been avoided, you know, if …

Captain: Your name, please.

Ethel: Ethel Swartzenberger. E-T-H-E-L-S ...

Captain: That's okay, ma'am. We'll look it up. Just tell me what you know.

Ethel: I've been around, Captain, and I happen to know people – what makes them tick and what makes them pop. And this kid definitely popped.

Captain: We've gathered that much, ma'am. Can you tell us anything specific?

Ethel: The kid's nutty.

Captain: The facts, lady. We only want the facts.

Ethel: Okay. You want facts? Try this on for size. The kid is sixteen years old, which automatically makes him a juvenile delinquent. If you ask me, children should be locked up between the ages of ten and eighteen. We wouldn't have near the problems in this world if we could rid ourselves of these mouthy youngsters. You know what I mean?

Huh? Huh?

Captain: Sergeant, get rid of this woman. Lock her up, put a gag in her mouth. Something.

Sergeant: Right, sir. This way, ma'am.

Peterson: Captain, here are the kid's parents. (**Ralph** *and* **Judy** *enter with* **Peterson**.)

Judy: What's going on? What's happened? Where are my children?

Captain: Both your children are in the house.

Judy: Are they hurt? Oh, I knew we shouldn't have gone out tonight.

Captain: No, they're not hurt.

Ralph: Then what is it? Who's in charge here?

Captain: You're talking to him, Mr. Miller. I'm Captain Davis.

Ralph: Well, Captain, what's going on? What's happened to our children?

Captain: Nothing's happened to them ... so far.

Judy: (*becoming hysterical*) Someone's in there. They've been kidnapped, haven't they? How much do they want? Tell them they can have everything we own.

Ralph: Judy, will you get a hold of yourself? Let the Captain talk. Well, Captain, what is it?

Captain: Mr. and Mrs. Miller, this is the situation. Your son is holding your daughter hostage, demanding that you be located and brought here. That's all we know up to now.

Judy: (**Judy** and **Ralph** *look at each other then at the* **Captain**) What kind of joke is this? Is this their idea of a fun evening? What have I been telling you, Ralph? You need to start putting your foot down with them. What are the neighbors going to say? We'll be the laughingstock of the town.

Captain: Ma'am, I assure you this is no joke. Your son called us at headquarters at approximately twenty-one-hundred hours, informed us that he was holding his sister at gun point and demanded that you be found and brought here immediately.

Judy: Well, for heaven's sake, what for?

Captain: I was hoping you could tell me.

Ralph: Well, there's only one way to find out. I'm going in there.

Captain: I wouldn't do that if I were you, Mr. Miller.

Ralph: Why not?

Captain: Because the situation at this point is uncertain. We've told him we're here and that we're looking for you. He told us to stay away until you arrived. He sounds pretty panicky. I wouldn't want to assume anything with your daughter in there with him.

Ralph: All right, Captain, we'll play it your way – *for now*. Let's tell him we're here.

Captain: (*picks up megaphone*) Tom! Tom Miller! Can you hear me? (*waits. No response*) We have located your parents. They're here now. (*to* **Ralph**) Mr. Miller, why don't you say something so he knows you're here.

Ralph: Boy, will I? (*grabs megaphone*) Listen, buddy …

Captain: (*grabs megaphone*) Mr. Miller, please. I know you're angry, but at this point we don't know who we're dealing with.

Ralph: All right. (*in megaphone*) Hello, Tom. This is your father. You want to tell me what's going on?

Judy: (*leaning to talk in megaphone*) And this is your mom, dear. We're here and we love you.

Ralph: Speak for yourself.

Captain: Quiet, everyone. He's com-ing out the door. (**Tom** *enters from opposite side of the stage holding* **Missy** *at gunpoint*)

Ralph: Now let me at him.

Captain: Mr. Miller, please.

Tom: Dad. Mom. Move out in front so I can see you.

Judy: Oh, Ralph. Where'd we go wrong?

Ralph: Okay, Tom, we're here. Why don't you put the gun down so we can relax and talk easier?

Tom: Oh, no you don't. First we talk.

Judy: Tom, dear, we're right here, all ears. Whatever you want.

Ralph: Judy!

Judy: Well, Ralph, what could the boy want that could be that bad?

Tom: All right, here it is. (*gets piece of paper out of his pocket*)

Captain: (*to crowd*) Shhhh.

Tom: I've had it, you hear? I can't take it anymore with the way things are. I don't know where I'm headed or where I even want to go. And you guys are no help. Dad, you're always working; you're never at home anymore. And school isn't any good. I'm just tired of the ways things are, so I've decided that I'm going to get what I want out of life – starting with number one: I don't ever have to do one more job around the house.

Ralph: (*disbelief*) What?!

Tom: Number two: I want to come and go as I please. Number three: I get twenty dollars allowance every week or whenever I need it. Number four: I get my own TV, disc player, phone, video, and car. Number five: I sleep as late as I want and then go to school. Number six: I don't show for family gatherings. Number seven: a case of Dew and fresh Nachos available at all times. Number eight: when my friends come over, you disappear. Number nine: I don't ever baby-sit this thing again. (*pushes **Missy** away, who then runs to **Judy's** arms*) And finally, number ten: the right to add more demands to these demands at any time.

Judy: Is that all dear? (**Ralph** *gives her a dirty look.*)

Tom: Yeah.

Captain: (*to **Ralph** and **Judy***) Well, I would suggest you meet his demands.

Ralph: Now I know this is a set-up.

Captain: What I mean, sir, is that if you verbally submit to your son's demands, we can get his gun, and then you can deal with him as you see fit before we take him in.

Ralph: Sorry, but I don't cater to my children's demands. This kid has gone way out of line this time. He's not only disobeyed his parents, and threatened his sister, but he has broken the law. I will not tolerate this behavior. I'm bringing this charade to an end. (*heads towards* **Tom**)

Judy: Ralph, come back.

Captain: Be ready to shoot when I say the word. (**Officers** *move up to the front with hands on their guns*)

Tom: Dad, don't come any further. Please, don't make me do this.

Ralph: Tom, I can't let you get away with this.

Tom: I'm warning you, Dad.

Captain: Get ready! (**Officers** *raise their guns*)

Ralph: Son, give me the gun.

Tom: No, Dad.

Ralph: The gun!

Tom: No!

Captain: Aim! (**Officers** *aim their guns*)

Judy: Ralph! Tom!

Missy: Daddy! (**Ralph** *goes for the gun*)

Tom: (*screams*) Nooooo!

(*At this point, everything and everyone moves in slow motion.* **Tom** *shoots several squirts from a water pistol.* **Ralph** *gets it in the face, attempts to block the stream of water, then brushes water away from his face with the back of his hand.*)

Ralph: (*breaking the moment*) A water pistol! (*The* **Crowd** *all gasp and begin murmuring.* **Tom** *smiles as if to make light of the situation.* **Ralph** *is barely able to contain his anger.*) If you know what's good for you, you'll run as fast as you can to the police or your mother, because in about one second I'm going to lose control and possibly hurt you permanently. (**Tom** *runs from* **Ralph** *and hides behind* **Judy**.)

Judy: Oh, no, you don't. I'm not protecting you from your father this time.

Captain: Listen, I don't want any more trouble.

Ralph: All I want is an explanation, then he's all yours, Captain.

Tom: (*starts out slowly and cautiously, but works up his courage*) Well, for sixteen years I've been doing what you want, and lately I've been getting pretty frustrated. I've been really tense, so I decided that I needed a change. I mean, it's only fair. But you never listen to me. So I thought this would be a creative way to get your attention. I just thought that maybe if I could have some things my way, then I'd be a lot happier.

Ralph: Well, Son, you definitely got my attention. And I'm sorry I haven't been around for you. But this was wrong. I'm not going to meet your demands. At least not all of them; at least not now. Take him away, officer.

Captain: Come on, kid.

Discussion Questions

1. What demands do your parents place on you? Are they fair or unfair? Why?
2. What creative or traditional ways have you tried to get their attention?
3. If you had a wish list, what "demands" would you make of your parents? Would they possibly negotiate some?
4. In Luke 15:11-32 Jesus tells the parable of the prodigal son. How do you think your parents would react if you left home? Then came back?
5. What needs and wants do your parents meet?

STORY OF LITTLE JOE

(Genesis 37-45)
Sharon Sherbondy

Characters
Narrator offstage voice
Little Joe farm boy
Hoss farm brother
Bobby farm sister
John farm brother
Billy farm sister
Chorus all the cast

All the cast *are standing in a line facing the audience, dressed in overalls and straw hats.* **Little Joe** *is wearing a bright coat over his overalls.*

Narrator: There once was a man named Idaho who had many, many kids.

Hoss: I'm Hoss.

Bobby: I'm Bobby.

John: I'm John.

Billy: I'm Billy.

Narrator: But his most prized and favorite child was a boy named Little Joe.

Chorus: (*Sing the first part of the theme song from* Bonanza.)

Narrator: Now when Little Joe went to sleep at night …

Chorus: (*snoring sounds, leaning on each other*)

Narrator: He had strange and wondrous dreams.

Chorus: (*dreamlike movements*) Oooooo, ahhhhhh.

Narrator: He shared those dreams with his family one day.

Joe: Hey, guys, listen to this: I had a dream that while we all were working on the farm, you all's haystacks got up and bowed down to mine. Then I had 'nother dream the very next night, wheres the sun, moon, and all them stars came and bowed down to me, too. Ain't that a kick?

Narrator: Well, the kids weren't too thrilled with this news from Little Joe, so they stripped him of his coat and threw him in a well.

Chorus: (*While singing "da-da-da" to the stripper song,* **the rest of the cast** *push* **Little Joe** *and take off his coat.*)

Narrator: Then along came a senator …

(**John** *becomes the senator and holds his overall straps as if it were a vest.*)

… with connections at the top, looking to hire some kid cheap to help him with his work.

Bobby: (*in Mae West style to* **Little Joe**) Hey, big fella, why don't you come on up and see us sometime?

Narrator: So the kids went home to Dad with a blood-stained, ripped-up coat and told him that an animal had eaten Little Joe.

Chorus: (*arms linked*) "Lions and tigers and bears, oh, my. Lions and tigers and bears, oh, my."

Narrator: Meanwhile, Little Joe was working his way right up to the top.

Chorus: (*singing*) "On top of Old Smokie …"

Narrator: The top of the political world, that is. He had become the expert in the field of food and farm land. Back at the farm, everything was going on as usual until one day a disaster came along unannounced.

Chorus: (*making blowing sounds and swaying their bodies*)

Narrator: The farm was destroyed along with their home and food.

Chorus: (*crying on each other's shoulders*)

Narrator: However, there came a report from Washington that food and money was available to all who came and picked it up.

Chorus: (*whistles and cheers*)

Narrator: So off the kids went to Washington to get a second start in life.

Chorus: (*arms linked, singing*) "We're off to see the Wizard, the wonderful Wizard of Oz."

Narrator: They had vowed that they would fulfill their promise to their dad to return with all the food they needed.

Bobby: (*rhythmically, with a cocky and confident voice*) I'm going to bring home the bacon. Fry it up in a pan.

Narrator: Little did they know as they walked up to the steps to the White House …

Chorus: (*turns and tiptoes in place.*)

Narrator: … that they would come face to face with a nightmare from the past.

Chorus: (*gasping and falling backwards into each other's arms*)

Narrator: The man that they had traveled over miles and mountains to see was Little Joe, as big and bright as day, wearing a suit and tie and black-framed glasses. Well, the kids immediately began to make out a will and testament.

Chorus: (*right hands raised*) "I, hereby, do solemnly swear to leave all my U2 tapes to my friends."

Narrator: The kids then began to beg for pardon and forgiveness for their past treatment of their little brother.

Chorus: (*bowing down to **Little Joe***) Please, let us live. Have mercy on us ignorant, stupid, rotten, unloving, jealous …

Joe: All right. All right.

Narrator: Said Little Joe. The kids were soon to find out that Little Joe was not the man that they had guessed him to be. Instead of life in prison or hanging from a tree which they deserved …

Chorus: (*to narrator*) Shhhh.

Narrator: … Little Joe forgave them and loved them.

Chorus: (*everyone hugs each other*)

Narrator: Little Joe bought them a condominium in Florida, a ranch in Wyoming, several BMWs, and everything else they needed.

Chorus: Why?

Joe: Why? Because I love you.

Chorus: (*looking lovingly and gratefully at* **Little Joe** *as they sing*) M-O-U-S-E.

Narrator: Well, the kids were a happy family for the first time in their lives …

(**Little Joe** *moves to center of group.* **All** *stand with arms around each other.*)

… all because Little Joe had shown them great love and mercy. So, with Wyoming in mind, they packed up their belongings and headed down the trail to a full life and a bright new future.

Chorus: (*turning and singing*) "Happy trails to you, until we meet again." (*to audience*) "You all come back now, you hear?" (*whistling "Happy Trails" as they walk offstage*).

Discussion Questions

1. In your opinion, why was Little Joe so gracious to his brothers?
2. Why is admitting wrong and asking forgiveness so hard?
3. When is forgiving hard?
4. Who do you find it easier to ask or give forgiveness to, friends or family? Why?
5. Jesus says in Matthew 5:24 that before we come before him we are to work things out with people we're not getting along with. What relationships in your life need some work?

Tough Issues

SCARS

Debra J. Poling

Characters

Tony sensitive seventeen-year-old

Gwen sixteen, fairly well adjusted, considering traumatic childhood

Mom Gwen's forty-five-year-old mom

Stage left is doorway from outside entering into Gwen's living room where her **Mom** *sits reading a book.* **Tony** *and* **Gwen** *are standing outside of Gwen's front door. It is at the end of their fifth or sixth date.*

Tony: As usual, Gwen, I had a great time.

Gwen: Me too, Tony. You were pretty good on those skates – once you got the hang of it.

Tony: (*rubbing his rear*) I think I stopped falling out of necessity.

Gwen: Well, I better go in.

Tony: (*taking hold of* **Gwen's** *hands*) Are we on for next Saturday?

Gwen: (*visibly uncomfortable at* **Tony's** *touch*) Ah … sure. Next Saturday would be fine.

Tony: Great. (*moving in as if to kiss* **Gwen. Gwen** *pulls away*) What's the matter with you? (*lightly*) Do I need a sparkling drop of retsin or something?

Gwen: No … no … it's not that at all.

Tony: Well, what's wrong? It's not too forward to give a quick kiss good night, is it?

Gwen: Well, no.

Tony: We have been dating pretty often. I just want to show a little affection.

Gwen: I know.

Tony: (*getting a bit mad*) You push away from me even just holding your hand. Are you leading me on, Gwen?

Gwen: Tony, I really enjoy being with you. I look forward to our dates.

Tony: Well then, what's wrong? I'm not asking to go to bed with you!

Gwen: Can we talk about this some other time? It's really late, and I'd better get inside.

Tony: Yeah, only we *are* going to talk about this. I gotta know why you don't even want me to touch you! Gwen, I care about you.

Gwen: (*entering the house*) Goodnight, Tony.

Tony: (*dejected*) Goodnight, Gwen. (*exits*)

Mom: (*looking up from the paper*) Hi, Honey. How was your date?

Gwen: (*trying to hide how upset she is*) Oh, it was fine. I really like Tony.

Mom: He seems like a real nice guy.

Gwen: Yeah, he's real nice. (*begins to cry quietly*)

Mom: Honey, what's wrong?

Gwen: Oh, Mom, you know we've been dating for a while, and well, I just can't relax when he touches me.

Mom: (*suspiciously*) How does he want to touch you?

Gwen: Not like *that!* He just wants to hold my hand. Tonight he wanted to give me a kiss good night, and I just couldn't let him get close.

Mom: What are you feeling when he gets close?

Gwen: (*hesitantly*) Scared … real scared.

Mom: (*Pause*) Do you think of Uncle Joe?

Gwen: (*wringing her hands*) I've tried not to. I've tried so hard, but those memories just flood back into my mind. I thought when I was finally able to tell somebody what he was doing to me that everything would be fine. And then when he went to jail, I thought the fears would go away. But Mom, I'm so afraid of any guy touching me. I just can't stand it. Am I ever going to be normal?

Mom: Gwen, you experienced a horror that no child should ever have to live through. It's going to take a long time to get over this. (*drawing **Gwen** gently to her*) Honey, I wish I could just erase the memory from your mind, but I can't.

Gwen: I wish someone could take the memories away.

Mom: You know it helps to talk about it. Have you told Tony yet?

Gwen: Are you crazy? He'd never want to see me again. He'd think I was … you know … used!

Mom: You're going to have to tell him something. I think he's a pretty sensitive guy. He may not fully understand, but I'm sure he wouldn't reject you. Gwen, what your Uncle did to you was not your fault. You know that, don't you?

Gwen: I know that, but it's hard not to feel guilty anyhow.

Mom: Do you think you might want to talk to a counselor about this?

Gwen: A *shrink?* Mom, I'm not loony!

Mom: Honey, calm down. I suggested it only because someone trained in this kind of thing would probably be more helpful than I could be.

Gwen: I'm just starting to feel comfortable talking with you. Don't make me tell everything to a stranger.

Mom: I won't make you do anything, Gwen.

Gwen: Thanks, Mom. (**Mom** *and* **Gwen** *pause for a moment.*)

Mom: Well, I better get to bed. (*gets up to leave, then turns back*) Gwen?

Gwen: Yeah, Mom?

Mom: The memories will never go away completely. But they will fade. And you will enjoy being touched by others. (*hugs* **Gwen**)

Gwen: (*giving a half laugh*) At least I don't mind being touched by you.

Mom: Give yourself time. And let others help you. Good night, Honey.

Gwen: (*pauses*) Good night. Have a good sleep. (*sitting back in the chair with a sigh*) Please God, let me have a good sleep ... with no dreams.

Discussion Questions
(**NOTE:** Due to the nature of this sketch, the author suggests that the discussion take place in small all-male and all-female groups.)
1. How common do you think sexual abuse is?
2. If Gwen had told you about being sexually abused by her uncle, do you think you would have believed her? What makes a story like hers hard to believe?
3. What do you think a person who has been sexually abused needs from a friend? What would you do if your best friend told you tomorrow that he or she had been abused?
4. What do you think God's attitude is toward sexual abuse? (Ps. 97:10). What do you think he feels for the victims? (Matt. 12:20). What do you think he feels for the abusers?

NOTE: Most abuse victims have been threatened and are very hesitant to tell anyone about their abuse. Most also feel that they won't be believed. If you suspect someone has been abused, or if someone tells you that they have been abused, *believe them*! You may want to suggest they tell a church staff member, call a local abuse hot line, or contact the Department of Child and Family Services in your area. Or maybe you yourself have had Gwen's experience. Sexual abuse, whether you are a male or female, will affect your life even after the abuse stops. Tell a trusted person, and allow yourself to be given help. You deserve it. You are a treasure.

DEAR ANYBODY

Debra J. Poling

Characters

Eddie	sixteen years old, going through some rough times
Rebecca	sixteen years old, ex-girlfriend of Eddie
Mom	forty-five years old, nice but firm
Coach Philips	thirty years old, very enthusiastic, peppy type

Eddie *is sitting at his desk in his bedroom, stage right.* **Rebecca, Mom,** *and* **Coach Philips** *are standing stage left, with no scenery, lit with a tight spot.*

Eddie: (*speaking into a tape recorder, haltingly at first*) Dear ... um ... Dear Anybody ... I wanted to make this tape to try to get my..uh ... feelings out. I mean, I kinda want to try to explain what I ... ah ... think about some stuff so it's clear for whoever cares to know.

First of all, Rebecca, I just want you to know that I understand why you dumped ... I mean ... ended our relationship. I know I came on pretty strong. I guess I liked you more than you liked me.

Rebecca: (*spot up on* **Rebecca's** *face and shoulders*) I *like* you. It's just that we don't have much in common. You're more ... you know ... introspective. You take everything *so* seriously. I just want to be friends and have fun. We're too young to get so involved. Can't you lighten up a bit? (*lights out on Rebecca*)

Eddie: Lighten up a little. I can lighten up all you want, on the outside. But I thought you really wanted to get to know me ... under the surface ... like I wanted to know you. That's okay, Rebecca, I understand. I can't expect you to be the one who helps me work out all the junk in my life.

This brings me to you, Mom. I'm very happy for your new marriage to Jack. He seems like a good guy for you, and you seem to be happier than I ever remember you being – even before you and Dad started fighting all the time. You seem just like young newlyweds. I know you know it's hard for me to adjust to having Jack around, but I don't think you understand how hard it is to all of a sudden be a third wheel. You and I used to have some good times together. Now, it's either you and Jack, or you and Jack and me. I miss having you all to myself, Mom.

Mom: (*spot on* **Mom's** *face and shoulders*) Now Eddie, it's not that bad. A lot of kids have adjusted to having a stepfather. You can, too. Think of all the kids that have it worse than you! At least you have a stepfather who gives you whatever you need. Besides, Eddie, I've got to have a life of my own, too. Now snap out of this self-pity. You know I love you. (*lights out on* **Mom**)

Eddie: I think I'm living with self-pity because I'm not getting any pity from you. Mom, I don't want to be a burden. I don't want to be an emotional leech. I just need a little attention, a little bit of your time all to myself. But I understand you now have someone whom *you* love and who needs your attention. I understand, Mom. Coach Philips tells me to get off the self-pity trip, too.

Coach: (*spot on* **Coach Philips**, *face and shoulders only. He talks as if giving a pep talk.*) Eddie, you may never make the Olympic gymnastic team, but you could be a good vaulter if you put your mind to it. But your mind is occupied too much by your personal problems. You gotta put them out of your mind. Pretend like you have no problems and soon you won't. Concentrate on your vaulting and leave your petty problems behind, boy. You've got it no worse than any other kid. (*Lights out on* **Coach**)

Eddie: It's obvious that everyone thinks my problems aren't that bad, and since I can't get over them on my own, I'll get permanent, painless help.

Please don't be upset at this. Just think of it as the way I chose to cure myself. Soon you'll forget all about me. I'm sure we'll all be better off in the end. I'm really sorry for all the trouble I've caused. (*Lights fade out on* **Eddie** *as he leaves stage right. Lights come up half on* **Rebecca, Mom** *and* **Coach Philips** *as they all talk at the same time.*)

Rebecca: Eddie, you're a nice guy, but we just aren't compatible. You're too serious. Let's just be friends.

Mom: A lot of kids have it worse than you. You have a very generous stepfather. Think of me, Eddie. I have needs, too. I have a life to live, too.

Coach: Concentrate on your vaulting. Your problems aren't very serious. Just leave them behind. Forget about them and they'll go away.

(*After a few seconds of the unison talking, a gun shot is heard offstage.* **All** *three stop talking the instant the gun goes off. Lights fade slowly on* **Rebecca, Mom** *and* **Coach Philips**.)

Discussion Questions
1. Why do you think people commit suicide?
2. Do you think suicide is ever justified? Why or why not?
3. Do you think you'd ever get to the point of wanting to commit suicide? What would have to happen in your life for things to get so bad that you'd consider it? Where would you turn for help if you were considering suicide?
4. If you had a friend who told you he was thinking of suicide, what would you tell him? Is there anything you think would *not* be a good thing to say?
5. How do you think God feels about suicide? About the person considering or committing suicide?

THE REFUGEE

Debra J. Poling

Characters

Janie high-school student who has had to grow up too quickly because her father is an alcoholic

Linda naive high-school student from a good family

Set in Linda's bedroom about nine-thirty on a school night.

Linda: … so I folded the note up real small and passed it over to Sue.

Janie: What did she do when she read it?

Linda: She never got it. Just as I was handing it to her, Mr. Lewis saw what I was doing and grabbed it.

Janie: You're kidding!

Linda: No, I'm not. He unfolded it, started to read it to himself, and then took it up to the front of the class.

Janie: He didn't read it out loud, did he?

Linda: (*nodding her head*) The entire letter. The class was roaring. (*laughs*)

Janie: Weren't you dying of embarrassment?

Linda: Of course not.

Janie: But you said you wrote all about Philip and what a hunk you thought he was. I would've died on the spot.

Linda: So would've I … if anyone had known I wrote it.

Janie: Oh … I get it … you didn't put your own name on it.

Linda: Right. I put Beth's name on it!

Janie: She's gonna kill you.

Linda: Better she kills me than I die of embarrassment.

Janie: I guess so. By the way, what time is it?

Linda: Nine-thirty.

Janie: Oh man, I've got to call my mom and tell her I'll be late getting home. (*crosses to the phone.* **Linda** *sits back and listens while filing her nails.*) Hello, Mom? This is Janie … Is everything okay? You sound upset … Oh no, not again. Did he come home from work that way? … Where's Kelly? … Oh. Is she going to spend the night over there? … (*turning away from* **Linda**) Mom, I don't know if I can ask her. Linda doesn't know anything about Dad … He's that bad, huh? … Yeah, I'll see if I can stay here … What are you going to do? … Well, should I call someone for help? … Are you sure? … Okay. Just be careful. I'll see you after school tomorrow. Bye. (*hangs up*)

Linda: What was that all about?

Janie: Linda, we're having some … problems at home. Do you think your parents would mind if I stayed here tonight?

Linda: What kind of problems?

Janie: (*hesitantly*) Well, you see, my dad sometimes drinks too much and when he gets drunk he … kinda beats us up.

Linda: Are you kidding?

Janie: And when he gets like that Mom doesn't like us to be around, you know, for our own safety. So that's why I want to spend the night here.

Linda: I don't know. It is a school night. I don't know if my parents would understand. Won't your dad just eventually pass out?

Janie: (*trying to be patient with her lack of understanding*) He's not that kind of drunk. He gets real violent.

Linda: Come on, Janie, everybody's dad has too much to drink now and then.

Janie: This is different. My dad is an alcoholic.

Linda: (*flippantly*) So have him go to Alcoholics Anonymous.

Janie: (*getting angry*) He won't go to A.A. He won't even admit he's got a drinking problem.

Linda: You don't have to get mad.

Janie: This is why I never told you about this before. I knew you wouldn't understand.

Linda: Come on, Janie, what do you expect? You make it sound like you're living in some kind of TV drama – you know, the drunk dad who beats up his family.

Janie: Where do you think the writers of those TV shows get their material? Don't you see ... I live in one of those kinds of homes. (*beginning to break down*) Remember that time I came to school with a black eye and told everyone that I walked into a door?

Linda: (*surprised*) Your dad did that?

Janie: Yes. Most of the time he hits us in less obvious places.

Linda: Where have you gone before when this happened?

Janie: I usually sleep in my car.

Linda: Oh, Janie, I'm sorry. I just never thought these kinds of things happen to people I know.

Janie: Well, they do.

Linda: I'll be right back. I'm going to ask my parents about your sleeping over.

Janie: Are you going to tell them about my dad?

Linda: They're gonna want to know why you're staying over on a school night. Janie, I think they'll understand. (*exits*)

Janie: (*nervously pacing*) I am so stupid! Why did I ever tell Linda? I should've just slept in my car. They're not going to believe me. I'm so stupid.

Linda: (*enters*) They said you would be welcome to stay tonight ... and anytime you have to get out of the house.

Janie: They understood?

Linda: Yep. In fact, they want to talk to you about it.

Janie: (*angry*) Oh, that's just great. Now I've go to explain the whole thing to them. They'll probably tell me to take my dad to A.A. too.

Linda: Janie, my parents are real easy to talk to. And maybe it would help to be able to talk to an adult about it. They won't make you do anything.

Janie: *(hesitantly)* I guess it would be all right.

Linda: But first we've got to figure out what you can wear to school tomorrow.

Janie: Linda ... don't tell anyone at school, okay?

Linda: *(pause)* Are you afraid they would react like I did?

Janie: *(nods)*

Linda: I won't tell a soul. Now, come on, let's go look in my closet and find you something to wear. (*They exit.*)

Discussion Questions

1. Most people think of drinking as a way to loosen up and have fun. What are some of the *negative* ways alcohol can affect people?
2. Do you think people can just stop drinking if they want to? Why do you think people keep drinking even when it causes so many problems in their families and lives?
3. Why do you think a person like Janie wouldn't want to tell anybody about what was happening in her family?
4. What are some things you can do to help a friend if you find out that their family has problems related to alcohol? What are some things you think you *shouldn't* do?
5. Ephesians 5:18 says, "Do not get drunk ... which leads to debauchery" (NIV; NASB says "dissipation"). What does that word mean? (Use a dictionary if you need to.) How might getting drunk, even occasionally, lead to hardships?

CATCH 22

Sharon Sherbondy

Characters
Nancy   average high-school student
Chris   average high-school student

*Scene opens with **Nancy** in her living room gathering her schoolbooks together, looking through her notebook as if checking on the assignments.* **Chris** *enters.*

Chris: Hi.

Nancy: Where'd you come from?

Chris: Your mom let me in.

Nancy: Hey, I'm getting ready to go over to Mr. and Mrs. Barlow's to baby-sit. Want to come along?

Chris: No, thanks. I don't really feel like being with … anybody right now.

Nancy: Oh, oh. Sounds serious. What's Brian done this time?

Chris: (*half smiling*) What makes you think it's Brian?

Nancy: Well, isn't it?

Chris: Kinda.

Nancy: Don't tell me you two are breaking up again? (**Chris** *doesn't respond*) Chris, Chris, Chris, Chris, Chris. Will you two just make up your minds? Are you together or not?

Chris: I don't know.

Nancy: You two have been dating forever. Don't you guys know if you love each other or not?

Chris: Yeah, I love him.

Nancy: And does he love you?

Chris: Yes.

Nancy: So, what's the problem?

Chris: We just don't want to rush into anything.

Nancy: Right.

Chris: Besides, something has come up.

Nancy: Another girl?

Chris: No.

Nancy: Another guy?

Chris: No.

Nancy: Well, what then?

Chris: (*pause*) I'm pregnant.

Nancy: You're *what?* How the heck did that happen? (**Chris** *looks at her as if to say, "Give me a break."*) Well, I know how it happened, but how did it happen?

Chris: I don't know. How does it ever happen? We just got carried away by the moment – I don't know. We didn't, like, plan it.

Nancy: I can't believe it.

Chris: Neither can I. I really blew it this time, didn't I? And now I'm paying for it, (*begins to cry*) really paying for it.

Nancy: (*hugs* **Chris**) Chris, I'm sorry.

Chris: I feel so stupid. I should have known better. But, really, it wasn't like we did it every time we went out.

Nancy: I know.

Chris: It just makes me so mad. Some girls do it all the time. Me, I get carried away once … twice. It's just not fair.

Nancy: Some of us are more fertile than others, I guess.

Chris: What a claim to fame.

Nancy: Have you told Brian?

Chris: Yeah. (*reluctantly*) We're … uh, I'm going to get an abortion.

Nancy: What?! You can't!

Chris: Why not?

Nancy: Because it's not right, that's why.

Chris: Nancy, I don't care whether it's right or not. I have to get an abortion.

Nancy: What about keeping the baby?

Chris: Oh, yeah, right. First of all, I'm not ready to be a mother, and second of all, I don't want to be tied down. I want to do things, go to college … (*pause*) Plus, I'm a Christian. Being Christian and pregnant don't exactly go together.

Nancy: And Christianity and abortion do?

Chris: Come on, don't lay that guilt trip on me.

Nancy: Chris, I'm not trying to lay a guilt trip on you.

Chris: Right.

Nancy: I'm just trying to get you to think. I mean, you've obviously not thought this thing through. You're just going to run off and have this abortion, just because you want to go to college?

Chris: You are really something, you know that? You sit there and tell me that this has been some easy decision. Well, for your information, I've been going through hell. I've been thinking and crying and crying and thinking until my body aches. And I'm telling you, I don't have any choice.

Nancy: That's not true.

Chris: Nancy, open your eyes. Look around you. Do you think our friends would ever accept me and my pregnancy? No way.

Nancy: You don't know that for sure.

Chris: Okay. You're right. I don't know that. But I'm not willing or secure enough to put them to the test. I just know that I'd get this reputation and not fit in anymore.

Nancy: You know I wouldn't drop you.

Chris: I know *you* wouldn't, but I don't know about the others. And it's not just my friends. What about my family? Nancy, if I went through with this pregnancy, I could never face them. I don't know which would be worse – my mother's look of disgust or her look of humiliation.

Nancy: Chris, I think you're overreacting.

Chris: Nancy, you don't know them. They'd throw me out. And I couldn't take that. And then there's church. You think they're going to welcome me with open arms? Get serious. So, now are you convinced that I've thought about this?

Nancy: No.

Chris: No? What is with you? Are you so good and self-righteous that you don't even want to try to understand what I'm going through?

Nancy: Chris, I understand.

Chris: Yeah, right.

Nancy: But there's something you've not thought about.

Chris: Here we go. It's time for the sermon. I knew it would come.

Nancy: There's the guilt. (**Chris** *rolls her eyes*) The guilt that you're going to live with for the rest of your life.

Chris: I can't believe this. You'll make a great mother.

Nancy: Will you listen to me? (**Chris** *turns away*) I've had an abortion. (**Chris** *turns and stares at* **Nancy**) Last year when I was dating Derek. We'd had a really good time together and one thing led to another, and abracadabra, I'm pregnant. Two weeks later I had an abortion.

Chris: Did Derek know?

Nancy: Why do you think we're not dating anymore? We never really talked about it. Like you, I pretty much had my mind made up. But the one thing that I was totally … unprepared for was the guilt. The pamphlets didn't mention it; the counselors never talked about it – no one told me about the guilt and shame that I was going to live with for the rest of my life.

Chris: Why didn't you tell me?

Nancy: I was too scared. I felt too ashamed. (*begins to cry*) See, the other thing about it is that it's, like, a really lonely sin, but one that seems to be everywhere – on TV, on the radio, at the movies, in the papers ... at church.

Chris: Nancy, I'm sure God's forgiven you.

Nancy: Yeah, I guess I know that, but it's still hard for me to face him. Sometimes it feels like it happened just yesterday.

Chris: So if you had to do it all over again, you'd have the baby?

Nancy: (*pause*) To be really honest, I don't know. Because you're right about people and their opinions. You're damned if you do and damned if you don't. But there's one thing I do know and that is that if you do go through with the pregnancy, God will be there for you. (*pause*) So will you at least think about it?

Chris: Yeah. But if I decide to go ahead with the abortion?

Nancy: God loves you no matter what. And I'll be here no matter what. But if you decide to have the baby, I'll be here, too.

Chris: (*hugs* **Nancy**) Thanks. Hey, what time were you supposed to be at the Barlow's?

Nancy: Right now. I think I'd better call them.

Chris: I'd better get going.

Nancy: Call me later?

Chris: Yeah. See ya.

Nancy: See ya. (*goes to phone and dials*) Mrs. Barlow? Hi, this is Nancy. I'm sorry I'm late. I'll get there in about ten minutes. Okay. Bye. (*hangs up phone, stops, turns and slowly sits and picks up her books.* **Nancy** *sits there, holding books tightly to her, and gently begins to rock, looking very sad.*)

Discussion Questions
1. What do you think and feel about abortion?
2. If a friend told you she was pregnant or he had gotten his girlfriend pregnant, how would you react? What would you say?
3. If you got pregnant or got your girlfriend pregnant (and don't say it's not possible!), what would you be scared of? What would you do? Who would you talk to?

4. James 5:16 tells us to confess our sins to each other. How can you put that into practice?
5. In Matthew 7:1-6, Jesus tells us not to judge others because we ourselves sin. What do you need to start dealing with in your life?

WEEDING

Debra J. Poling

Characters
Gary   high-school boy
Harry   a fifty-ish garbage collector

In an imaginary garden **Gary** *is pulling up the last of the weeds and putting them into a real garbage bag that is full of junk.*

Gary: (*on his knees leaning over an imaginary garden. He talks right to the audience.*) Well, that does it. I finally got this old garden cleaned out. It took me a long time to get serious about clearing the weeds, but it's finally finished.

(*pulling a weed out of a pile of trash*) Take this weed for example: it started growing when I was seven. Mom began teasing me in front of all my friends because I was having a problem wetting the bed. The roots of this weed go deep. I've always had some anger toward her for that.
And see this one? (*holding up another weed*) This blew into my garden when Dad ran off with the neighbor's wife. It was actually better when he finally left – I didn't have to listen to Mom and him yelling at each other all the time. And this pile of trash – (*holds up a pile of dirty papers, apple cores, etc.*) this was thrown in here by Mr. Wilson, my history teacher, who delighted in announcing to the entire class which students failed his exams. He would call us members of the "Moron Club." I hate anything having to do with history to this day.

So, there it is, all the weedy memories and depressing junk finally out of the garden of my life. Now, I realize there are lots of holes remaining in the dirt. But I'd much rather have pockmarked ground. Anything to get rid of the weeds!

Harry: (*enters*) Hi there. Is this trash ready to go?

Gary: Oh, hi. Are you the garbage man?

Harry: We prefer to be called sanitation engineers.

Gary: Sorry. Yeah, this is the garbage.

Harry: There's quite a pile of trash here.

Gary: Yeah, well I guess some of us have had more than our share of hard knocks. But now it's all cleared out of my life and ready to be taken away.

Harry: (*pulls out a small pad of paper and writes on it*) Let's see — that's about thirty gallons of trash ... should take us about three days to recycle it. You'll get it back on Monday morning. (*hands* **Gary** *a slip of paper*) Here's your claim check.

Gary: Get it back? What are you talking about? I don't want this back!

Harry: But that's what we do with all the trash we get. We take it to the recycling plant, process it, and return it to the owner.

Gary: But you don't understand. I want this stuff out of my life for good.

Harry: That's out of the question. Our job is to take the trash and recycle it.

Gary: Well then, you must be the wrong trash collection company. I want permanent trash removal!

Harry: We're the only sanitation engineers around.

Gary: (*getting desperate*) Listen, all my life I've had to live with the hurts and pains of a rotten family. Now I finally take action to clear out the junk, and you tell me that I have to take it all back? I don't want to have this garbage in my garden anymore!

Harry: Okay, so if I take this garbage away what are you going to use for fertilizer?

Gary: Fertilizer?

Harry: Yeah, you know you can't grow good food without fertilizer.

Gary: I've got good seeds, and lots of water.

Harry: But you need fertilizer.

Gary: So, I'll go to K-Mart and get some.

Harry: They don't sell fertilizer for the kind of garden you're growing.

Gary: Well, where do I get fertilizer?

Harry: From the recycling plant.

Gary: Where you take my garbage?

Harry: You're a bright kid. We take the junk from your life and recycle it into usable fertilizer. All those experiences you've endured will make a great mulch.

Gary: There you go again. Don't you see ... I don't want any of those experiences to be a part of my life, my garden, or the food from my harvest.

Harry: I'm sorry, but those experiences are permanently a part of you. And no amount of denying them, or throwing them away can change that.

But the owner of the recycling plant can use those experiences to make your garden soil rich. You'll end up with all sorts of food to share with others who might need help.

Gary: I can't get rid of the weeds, then?

Harry: (*shakes his head, no*) But you can turn them into something useful, both for yourself and for others.

Gary: And Monday you're going to come back here and dump all this junk right back into my garden.

Harry: Yes, only it won't be junk anymore. It will be the very thing that gives you strength of character and the ability to sustain others who are being choked by weeds in their own lives.

Gary: I guess I've got no choice.

Harry: I don't *have* to take the weeds and junk away.

Gary: (*resignedly*) No, no, don't leave it here. That'd be a lot worse. Monday, huh?

Harry: (*nods, yes*)

Gary: Could you do me a favor? When you bring it back, could you dump it on my garden gently? I couldn't stand to get overwhelmed with the garbage again.

Harry: I'll pour it on slowly, and you won't have more to deal with than you are able to handle — the owner of the recycling plant guarantees it.

(**Harry** *picks up the trash bag and begins to carry it out.* **Gary** *bends over his imaginary garden looking forlorn.* **Harry** *sets the bag down and comes back to* **Gary**.)

Harry: When your garden is in full bloom, you will hardly ever remember the weeds. You just wait and see. *(Exits. Lights fade slowly.)*

Discussion Questions

1. We all have "old weeds," experiences in our childhood that come to mind occasionally and cause us to feel angry, sad, scared, etc. Think of one of those times and share it with the group. It doesn't have to be dramatic. The everyday happenings of life are usually the ones that really stay with us.
2. What feelings do you have when you remember that time? What feelings do you have toward the other people involved?
3. What ways have you tried to work through that bad experience? If you've just tried to forget about it, how has that resolved your feelings?
4. Galatians 6:2 says, "Carry each other's burdens" Why might talking to someone about your hurts be helpful?
5. The Bible says we are to tell God about the "weeds" in our lives (Ps. 55:22, 1 Pet. 5:7). What can God do to help?

PHILOSOPHY OF POPULAR THINKING

Debra J. Poling

Characters

Mr. Lewis	teacher in his early thirties – the girls love him, the boys want to be like him
Joe Stanford	senior, antagonistic toward the class and Mr. Lewis
Bill	senior, regular kid
Susie	senior, regular kid
Classmates	several other students

In a high school classroom, **Students** *are standing around waiting for* **Mr. Lewis** *to enter.*

Susie: I'm really looking forward to this class. Mr. Lewis has the most totally awesome eyes.

Bill: My brother had him last year. He told me he runs ten miles a day!

Joe: Big deal.

Susie: Ah, come on, Joe. Are you gonna give him a hard time?

Joe: Probably.

Bill: Susie, just ignore him. Look, here he comes. (**Students** *take their seats.*)

Mr. Lewis: (*warm and friendly*) I'd like to welcome you to this course called Philosophy of Popular Thinking.

Susie: (*dreamily*) Thank you, Mr. Lewis.

Mr. Lewis: (*nods to* **Susie**) It wasn't very long ago when I was your age. I remember feeling a restlessness inside. I felt there had to be more to life than I was experiencing. I wanted to be happy. Does anyone here yearn for true happiness? (**Students** *all raise their hands.*)

Joe: I know where you can get it! Alfred is selling little pink pills of happiness after school.

Susie: Shut up, Joe.

Mr. Lewis: I've spent a lot of time searching for happiness, and I've discovered a way to reach it. Are you interested?

All: (*at the same time*) Sure, yeah, show us!

Mr. Lewis: There are three simple yet profound steps to reach a state of ultimate happiness. First, I want you to close your eyes and relax. (**All** *do, except for* **Joe** *who watches everyone else.*) Now relax, relax ... feel your head start relaxing. Feel your arms relaxing. Let all of your body relax, way down to your toes ...

Joe: (*loudly*) Susie, relax your own toes, not mine!

Susie: I didn't touch you! (**Students** *laugh*)

Mr. Lewis: People, don't lose your concentration. Sit back, relax, relax. The second step to ultimate happiness is in how you breathe. I want you to breathe in two short breaths (*demonstrates*) and then out one long, raspy breath. (*breathes out.* **Students** *try to hold back laughter.*)

Joe: Mr. Lewis, this is stupid. Relaxing and breathing like an elephant doesn't bring happiness.

Mr. Lewis: (*beginning to get angry*) Mr. Joseph Stanford, who do you think you are? You are not particularly bright or well liked. I am offering happiness to a roomful of people who want it. I would think you, more than any here, would want that also. Now, I suggest you sit down, shut up, and breathe so we might learn about the secret to happiness. (**Students** *cheer.*)

Now, everyone breathe with me: two short breaths in, one long breath out. (**Students** *all do it together, including* **Joe.**) Very good, class.

You are ready to learn the most important step, the step that will bring total happiness. The secret to total happiness lies in making the Ancient Poultry Chant. (*sounding like a chicken*) Braack, braack.

(*A few **students** begin to giggle, but the rest are very serious and tell the others to shut up.*)

Mr. Lewis: Now, you try it with me. (**Students** *do*.) Now whenever you get unhappy, just make the Ancient Poultry Chant.

All: Brraacckk, bak, bak, brraacckk!

Mr. Lewis: Your dad won't let you have the car Friday night!

All: (*getting more into it*) Brraacckk, bak, etc.

Mr. Lewis: Can you feel it helping? Aren't you happy?

All: Braackk, bak, etc.

Mr. Lewis: When something terribly awful happens, it is helpful to stand in the Ancient Poultry Position while doing the Ancient Poultry Chant.

(**Mr. Lewis** *stands, moving about and sounding like a chicken. Some of the* **Students** *do it with him.*)

Mr. Lewis: Imagine your dog just died. What do you do?

All: (*moving and sounding like chickens*)

Mr. Lewis: You just failed your college entrance exams.

All: Braacckk, bak, etc.

Mr. Lewis: You all look like fools.

All: Braacckk, bak, etc.

Mr. Lewis: I mean it, you all look ridiculous.

All: (*beginning to listen, but still doing the chicken noises and movements*)

Mr. Lewis: This is a joke, a farce.

All: (*slowly beginning to sit down, stunned*)

Mr. Lewis: Really, this is a joke. You

fell for a joke!

Joe: (*angrily*) You made us look like fools!

Mr. Lewis: You're right!

Susie: Of all the embarrassing tricks!

Bill: I'm dropping this class. Philosophy of Popular Thinking stinks!

Joe: Me too! And Lewis, you are a jerk!

Susie: Why did you do this to us?

Mr. Lewis: You really want to know?

Joe: No, Lewis! I'm sick of you.

Mr. Lewis: (*taking command*) This class is called Philosophy of Popular Thinking, right?

All: Yeah, so what?

Mr. Lewis: There are hundreds of people out there who are going to try to capture your mind, just like I did today. You must learn how to think critically – to not believe every philosophy that sounds like fun. You're going to have to learn how to test other people's opinions so that you will choose what's right, and not just what feels good.

Joe: Ah, come on, Mr. Lewis. You screamed at me to do this. I had no choice.

Mr. Lewis: And if I could convince you as easily as I did, think of someone who is serious about what they believe, and not just playing a joke. I'm sorry for embarrassing any of you. But I'd much rather have you be made a fool of here in class than out in the real world where it won't be a joke. Class dismissed. (**All** *exit except for* **Joe, Bill**, *and* **Susie**)

Susie: What a class!

Bill: It's spooky how easy it was to believe he really meant it.

Joe: I know. But I'm still ticked off at him for making us look like fools.

Susie: (*nudging* **Bill**) Well, you know how to get rid of that anger, don't you? (**Susie** *and* **Bill** *start acting like chickens and chase* **Joe** *off-stage.*)

Discussion Questions

1. What are some messages we hear that tempt us to believe things that are not necessarily true? (for example, commercials, lyrics in popular songs). How do you and your friends respond to these?
2. Think about a time you fell for a line that turned out to be far from true. How did you feel after you discovered the truth?
3. Jesus says we are to be "as shrewd as snakes and as innocent as doves" (Matt. 10:16). What does that mean? Substitute "wise" for "shrewd" and "gentle" for "doves." How does a person get wisdom?
4. How can we know if what we are being told is true? Read 1 John 4:1-3.
5. What are some things we can do to protect ourselves from getting caught up in believing ideas that are not true?

J.B.

(Job)

Sharon Sherbondy

Characters

Narrator   offstage voice
J.B.   average high-school student
Friends 1-4   know-it-alls

*Scene opens with two chairs placed center stage. As narration begins, **J.B.** enters and mimes what is being said about him.*

Narrator: Once upon a time in the land of US — that's spelled U-S — there lived a guy whose name was J.B. This guy was honest, sinless (well, almost), loved God, and hated evil. He had a letter sweater, was president of the senior class, was voted most likely to succeed, dated the best-looking girl in the school, drove a BMW, and owned two Harley Davidsons. He was the most popular guy in high school. One day after returning home from school, where he had just led the football team to victory, he found a note addressed to him on the living room chair.

J.B.: (*picking up note and reading aloud*) "Dear J.B.: We received a call from your principal tonight. He said, because of reasons un-mentioned, he wants you to turn in your letter sweater, Mary Jones has been appointed senior class president, your name has been removed from the yearbook, and you have been voted class jerk. Your girlfriend also called and said she's breaking up with you to go out with Wally." (*to audience*) Yuck! (*reading note again*) "Love, Dad. P.S. While you were gone tonight, some-one broke into the garage and stole your BMW and replaced your Harleys with Hondas."

Narrator: J.B. was devastated. He

had lost everything. He immediately knelt down on his knees and began praying.

J.B.: Dear God – my life is yours. Everything I had you gave to me, so you have every right to take it back. May I always continue to praise your name. Amen.

Narrator: As J.B. arose from prayer, he was suddenly struck with a terrible illness. He fell into the chair in great pain, moaning and groaning.

(**Friends 1-4** *enter miming the narrator's description.*)

At that moment four of J.B.'s friends walked in laughing and talking. All of a sudden they saw J.B. They immediately ran to his side.

1: J.B., what's wrong?

2: You look terrible. Are you sick?

3: When did this happen?

4: Should we call a doctor?

J.B.: If you guys will stop talking for a second, I'll tell you. Everything has happened. I'm sick, I no longer own my letter sweater, Mary Jones is now president of the senior class, I'm class jerk, my girl is dating Wally …

1-4: (*to audience*) Yuck!

J.B.: … my Harleys are Hondas, and my car has been stolen.

1-4: Your BMW?

J.B.: Yes, my BMW.

1-4: (*simultaneously pulling away from* **J.B.**) Oh, wow.

J.B.: I don't know why this is happening to me. I haven't done anything to deserve this. Oh, I wish I were dead. I wish I had never been born. I knew someday something terrible would happen. But why me? Why now?

1: Hey, wait a minute. You're the one who is always preaching at everyone to be strong and faithful when things get tough. And look at you. You're a bowl of Jell-O. The first sign of a little rough water and you're ready to end it all. Obviously, God is doing this to you to make you strong so you can start practicing what you preach.

J.B.: You're condemning me because I'm expressing a little misery?! Aren't I allowed to hurt and feel pain and loss? I just want to know why God is doing this to me.

2: I was always told that the reason people get sick or get in trouble is that they are sinning and refuse to change. Like Joni Eareckson Tada. She's got some sin that she's holding onto. It beats me why she just doesn't confess her sin so she can walk again. Pretty stubborn and stupid if you ask me.

J.B.: Nobody asked you, and anyway I *have* confessed everything. I've done no

wrong. Explain to me why some people, like movie stars who aren't Christians, are rich and famous. If what you say is true, then they should be sick and poor, not me.

3: Forget God, man. This God of yours doesn't sound too smart or loving. Why does he let people fight and die? Why does he cause earthquakes and famine? Your prayers aren't getting you anywhere, pal. If I were you, J.B., I'd go find me a God who cares about people. At one time I was thinking about becoming a Christian because you seemed so happy and lucky. But look at you. Where is God now?

J.B.: (*sarcastically*) You guys are a great comfort. Great friends. I can't tell you how much better I feel since you've come.

2: J.B. …

J.B.: I mean it. I'm telling you, I haven't done anything to deserve this. I love God and I will continue to praise him. I just want to know what's happening. Listen, I don't go to porno flicks, my morals are straight, I've never cheated in school or stolen anything. I share everything I have. Oh, God, talk to me. Where are you?

1: J.B., I'm telling you, this is God's will. He's doing this because you need to grow.

2: (*to* **1**) And I'm telling you he has been hiding something from God. God is punishing him so he will give in to him.

3: Forget God. He's not even paying attention to you or anyone. If this is what God is like, forget Christianity.

1-4: (*arguing over* **J.B.***, trying to prove themselves the wisest*)

Narrator: And so they argued among themselves, each one believing he had the answer until ...

4: Hey, wait a minute. Will you guys stop it? *Shut up*! Thank you. I can't believe my ears. You should hear yourselves. What a sad, sorry group of friends you are. (**J.B.** *nods in agreement.*) I'm talking about you, too, J.B. Who are you to question God? Are you as great, as all-knowing as God himself? Does he always fill you in on everything he does? What kind of leader are you? And you three – suddenly the experts on theology. "God's doing this to make you strong, J.B." "God's doing this because you've been bad, J.B." "Forget God, J.B." You should all get on your knees right now and ask God's forgiveness.

I mean, we're just people. How can we understand what God is thinking or doing? Can any of you explain how God created the earth, the snow, rain, hail? Were you there with him when he made the mountains and the valleys? Can you explain a sunset, a sunrise? Did you create life? He is the Almighty, the All Powerful. And you fools stand around as if you and God are one. God forgive you all.

J.B.: (*ashamed*) You're right. I was very wrong. I had no right to demand answers from God.

1: I was wrong, too. J.B., will you forgive me?

2: Me, too, J.B.?

3: I was the worst of all. I turned away from God.

All: (*on their knees together facing audience*)

Narrator: And so our story comes to an end. But life goes on for J.B. and his four friends. J.B. will soon get back his letter sweater, and his position as class president will be restored. His car was found with only a few dents in it, and he was able to find some sucker, er, I mean, guy to buy his Hondas so he could buy two new Harleys. But as for his girl, on the night of the prom she ran off with Wally.

All: (*to audience*) Yuck!

Discussion Questions
1. Why did J.B. have all his problems?
2. Why do you think they all blamed God?
3. What advice would you have for J.B.?
4. With whom did you identify with the most – J.B. or friend 1, 2, 3, or 4? Why?
5. What unanswered questions do you have? Talk about them.

Self-Image

LONELINESS

Sharon Sherbondy

Characters

Boy 1   **Boy 2**
Girl 1   **Girl 2**   **Boy or Girl 3**

Stage is set with two stools, one on each end of the stage. Begin with **Boy 1** *and* **Girl 1** *on the stools. As each person finishes the monologue, he or she walks to the back of the stage, and the next person sits down. The last person stands center stage. Lighting only on the person talking. Rest of stage remains black.*

Boy 1: I've been alone most of my life. From the time I was born I was in day-care. My parents both work, and sometimes I get angry. I come home from school to an empty house and stay all alone until around seven o'clock when my mother comes home from work. I watch TV, but after a while that gets pretty boring. So I

start to daydream – about having friends over or about getting into trouble.

Sometimes I like being alone. But it's a strange feeling. You're there all by yourself. You've got nobody to talk to. When my mom comes home, it's just as bad because when she comes in, she's tired and she goes to sleep. I try talking to her, but it's no use. I don't know … we just don't relate.

Girl 1: I think the reason I feel lonely is, well, you can't have friends if you don't like yourself. And I guess I don't like myself a whole lot. When I first meet someone, I'm always afraid that I'll say something stupid or do something wrong. And so I just don't talk and make friends, and that's why I guess I'm pretty lonely. See, I was going with this guy for two-and-a-half years, and while I was seeing him, I didn't really have any other friends. But then I broke up with him, and it was really hard to get back in with people. I couldn't go back to my old group be-cause, well, we hadn't hung around together for two-and-

a-half years. So here I am.

Boy 2: My dad's a CEO for this big company. I hardly ever see him. He spends more time at work than he does at home. And what's even worse is that this job is always moving us around. This is the sixth place I've lived in the past seven years. Almost every year we gotta move. I remember the first time we moved. I cried and cried and cried. I begged my parents to let me stay with my friends, but they made me come and promised me that I'd meet new friends that were just as nice.

Well, they were right. I did. But then I was scared that I'd have to leave them, too. And sure enough, I did. And again I cried, but this time I was cry-ing not just because I had to leave my friends, but because I was so angry at my parents. They couldn't have cared less that I was hurting. They had each other – or my mom had my dad, and my dad had his job. But I had no one. They didn't know and weren't in-terested in how hard it was to go to a new school where kids already had their friends. Everybody except me.

Every time I'd try to tell my parents how I felt, they'd either give me money or buy me something – like that took care of everything. Well, I'll tell you something. I don't cry anymore. Yeah, we still move a lot. But I quit making friends. I'm what you call a loner. Being a loner guarantees me a pain-free existence. Existence – that's about all it is, too.

Girl 2: When I was twelve my mom and dad got divorced. My mom had a hard time handling me – or so she said – so she sent me to live with my aunt for a while. I don't know why I couldn't have gone to live with my dad, except my mom told me he didn't want me – but I couldn't believe that 'cause we always got along.

After a while my mom met this man and got married, so I'm back living with her now. It's not much better. Sure, we do things together, but it's just not like it was when Mom and Dad were married. I just kinda feel like I don't belong. I visit my dad once in a while, but I don't belong there either. As much as I hated Mom and Dad fighting all the time, at least we were a family. Now we're nothing. My mom's got her new husband, and my dad's got his new wife. But what do I have? Where do I fit in?

**Boy/
Girl 3:** I've seen many friends come and go in my life, and lately I've learned a lesson about people – what used to be a shoulder to lean on is now sometimes just thin air. You see, I've longed to be the center of someone's universe, with all their cares and concerns orbiting nicely around me. But I've found that no one can fill that big a bill. No one devotes his entire life to the well-being of someone else. No one only human, that is.

That leaves open one possibility – one that is often too easily forgotten. (*pause*) Jesus – the perfect union of man and God. As a man – fully acquainted with joy and pain. As God – fully able to mold worthless junk into timeless treasure. He makes no unreasonable demands on me and sounds no alarms when I turn my back on him. Instead, he's a quiet, constant presence in my life. And he knows me better than anyone else.

It's funny, but I am the center of his universe and he longs to be the center of mine. Jesus, God, and friend. Faithful, devoted, everlasting – in whose presence we are never alone.

Discussion Questions

1. What kinds of things make you feel lonely? Why?
2. When was the last time you felt lonely?
3. When was the first time you felt lonely?
4. What do you usually do when you feel lonely?
5. What can you say or do for someone who tells you they feel lonely?

FEARFUL ASSUMPTIONS

Sharon Sherbondy

Characters

Roger   friendly seventeen year old
Meagan   insecure, frightened sixteen year old

**Aides One
and Two**   two hospital aides, dressed in white coats

Meagan *is sitting on a park bench with a blanket covering her lap and her hands. The only part of her body that moves is her head.* **Roger** *approaches carrying a sack lunch. He sees* **Meagan** *on the bench.*

    Roger: Mind if I sit here?

(**Meagan** *looks up nervously, but not at his face. She looks away quickly.*)

    Roger: (*pausing, looking puzzled*) No? Good. (*sits*)

(**Meagan** *looks away, showing extreme nervousness.*)

    Roger: (*opening a sack lunch, glancing at* **Meagan** *with a smile*) Nice day, huh?

(**Meagan** *shows fear.*)

    Roger: (*shrugging his shoulders, opens his lunch and takes a bite of his sandwich*) You must be new in town. I've never seen you around before.

(**Meagan** *doesn't respond.* **Roger** *shows frustration*)

    Roger: (*as if hit with a fresh idea*) You are new, huh? And you're thrilled to meet me? Why, thank you. I'm sorry, I didn't catch your name. Mary? That's a nice name. Do I always talk to girls I don't know? Not usually unless they look like they need a friend. (*pause*) So, Mary …

    Meagan: My name's not Mary.

    Roger: (*pleased with the results*) No? What is it, then?

    Meagan: Why should I tell you? I don't know you or anything about you. You could be a robber for all I know.

Roger: True, but I'm not. What would you like to know about me?

Meagan: (*scared*) Nothing.

Roger: Hey, listen, Mary …

Meagan: Meagan. (*pause*) My name's Meagan.

Roger: So, I was close.

Meagan: Well, don't come any closer.

Roger: Okay, I won't. (*thinking*) Well, like I said earlier, I've never seen you around before.

Meagan: Uh, my family just moved here.

Roger: Oh, so you'll probably be going to my high school. Have you been there yet? It's just right down the street.

Meagan: No, I don't go to school.

Roger: Oh. Why not?

Meagan: Because it's too … hard. I never did well. And plus high schools are so big, and there's so many people.

Roger: Yeah, I guess that can be kind of scary, but really, once you get in there and get involved …

Meagan: No, I'm fine right where I'm at.

Roger: Well, how about if I, at least, show you around? I could introduce you to some people.

Meagan: No, I don't want to meet people.

Roger: Hey, come on, it's no big deal; I don't mind. Besides, I know you'd really like my friends. In fact, there's going to be a party this weekend at my friend's house.

Meagan: No. I don't go to parties.

Roger: Now wait. This is just a party of about eight or ten of us.

Meagan: I said no! I get nervous at parties.

Roger: Well, how about if we go swimming? That might be more comfortable for you ...

Meagan: Swimming! People drown when they go swimming.

Roger: (*showing disbelief*) Okay. You don't like parties or people or swimming. What do you like to do?

Meagan: Nothing.

Roger: Nothing? No tennis, or card playing or ...

Meagan: Nothing!

Roger: That's too bad. You're missing out on life.

Meagan: Well, at least it's safer.

Roger: (*confused*) Yeah, I guess. (*pause*) So, if you're not going to go to school, are you going to work? What do you plan to do?

Meagan: I don't know. I don't want to think about it.

Roger: Meagan, what's with you? Why are you so scared of everything?

Meagan: I don't think it's any of your business. And besides, I'm not "scared of everything." I'm just ... careful. Say, why don't you just get lost?

Roger: I'm sorry, I'm just trying to help. Maybe you should talk to someone.

Meagan: Talk to someone! Listen, you, whatever your name is. Who do you think you are, talking to me like this? Why don't you just get out of here! There's nothing wrong with me. Did you ever think that it might be you that has the problem?

Roger: Listen, Meagan, really, I'm sorry. It's just that ...

Meagan: (*becoming panicked*) Hey, I gotta go. My friends are coming, and they'll probably want to sit here with me so if you could just, you know ...

Roger: (*looks behind him, puzzled*) Sure. Well, maybe I'll see you later.

Aide One: (*pushing a wheelchair*) Well, Meagan, you ready to go?

Meagan: (*embarrassed, nervous*) Yeah.

(**Aides** *get on each side of* **Meagan**, *pick her up, and place her in the wheelchair.*)

Aide Two: Here we go now. That's a good girl. We'll make it back to the hospital just in time for your afternoon nap.

(**Aide One** *rolls her away.* **Meagan** *avoids* **Roger**.)

Roger: (*grabbing* **Aide Two's** *arm*) Excuse me. But I had no idea. What's wrong with her?

Aide Two: Nothing, really.

Roger: What do you mean, nothing? She's in a wheelchair, isn't she? And she seems so frightened.

Aide Two: That's just it.

Roger: What's it?

Aide Two: All those fears of hers have put her in that wheelchair. They've crippled her — for life, probably.

Roger: For life? Well, can't you do anything for her?

Aide Two: Not until she's ready to face them. Until then, she's paralyzed. It's all up to her. (*walks away.* **Roger** *stands there in disbelief.*)

Discussion Questions
1. Why is it so hard to face our fears? What stops us?
2. What sort of things have you found to help you face your fears?
3. Have you ever tried to help someone who was afraid to let you? What did you do?
4. What are your worst fears?
5. What was Jesus afraid of in his life? How did he deal with his fears?

I AM JOE'S STOMACH

Debra J. Poling

Characters

Gut	the foreman of Joe's stomach, wearing a white shirt with pens in his chest pocket, blue pants, and a hard hat.
Amy and Andy Acid	workers in the stomach, wearing work clothes and hard hats and spending most of their time beating on a pile of "food" with bats, hammers, hatchets, etc.
Elaine & Ernie Enzyme	workers in work clothes, spending most of their time pulling on their pile of food (enzymes in the stomach pull protein out of food).
Two Tums	one or two people carrying oversized "Tums."

Gut *stands center stage. The* **Acids** *are stage left behind* **Gut***, pounding on their pile. The* **Enzymes** *are stage right pulling on their pile.*

Gut: (*talking to* **Elaine**) Well, if you can't handle the job alone, then get Ernie to help.

Elaine: But he's already working.

Gut: I don't want excuses. Now get to work. (**Elaine** *leaves absolutely defeated and forlorn.* **Gut** *notices the audience.*) Oh, hello there. I didn't see you come in. You've all heard of "I Am Joe's Brain" or "I am Jane's Heart." Well, I am Joe's Stomach. The gang around here just calls me Gut. The stomach is a fascinating organ. The way it can take anything the esophagus dumps in it and turn it into useful fuel is so ...

Amy: Excuse me sir, but we're having a problem with the acid flow.

Gut: Again? (*to audience*) Oh ... this is Amy, head of the acid department. Excuse me for a moment folks. (*to* **Amy**) Now what's wrong?

Amy: We can't seem to generate enough acid to break down the garbage – I mean, food – that esophagus is dumping in here.

Gut: Is everyone on duty now?

Amy: Yes, sir.

Gut: Well, then what's slowing things up?

Amy: Well, sir, Joe ate a sixteen-inch pepperoni pizza and two liters of coke at 2:00 A.M., and it kinda got stuck in the small intestine.

Gut: Why?

Amy: There seems to be a backup in the large intestine – a lot of, shall we say, air that needs to pass before we can move the pizza on down.

Gut: So what's that got to do with the current lack of help on the new supply of food?

Amy: Sir, half of our crew is down in the small intestine trying to break things up a bit more, and the esophagus just dumped Joe's breakfast down here.

Gut: (*sounding concerned*) The usual?

Amy: Yes. Two Suzy-Q's, Fritos, and hot cocoa.

Gut: (*grimacing*) I see. Just do the best you can.

Amy: Yes, sir. (**Amy** *goes back to* **Andy**, *and they resume pounding on the pile of* "*food*".)

Gut: Now, as I was saying, it's so thrilling the way the stomach can take anything – well, almost anything – and make it into useful fuel …

(**Gut** *is distracted by yelling and cheering and jumping around in the background. It's* **Ernie** *and* **Elaine** *having a sugar buzz.*)

Gut: What in the world is going on?

Ernie: (*running, jumping, carrying on*) Snack, sir.

Elaine: (*running in circles, bobbing her head rapidly*) Dun … Dun …

Gut: (*to audience*) Excuse this outburst folks. This is Elaine and Ernie Enzyme (**Ernie** *and* **Elaine** *wave*), and normally they are very sedate and careful workers. I don't know what …

Elaine: Dun … Dun …

Gut: Elaine, slow down. I can't understand what you're …

Elaine: Dunk … Dunk …

Gut: Dunk? What is Dunk?

(*Suddenly* **Elaine** *and* **Ernie** *go into extreme slow motion.*)

Elaine: (*talking very slowly*) Dunkin' Donuts!

(**Elaine** *and* **Ernie** *crash to the floor as if dead.*)

Gut: Dunkin' Donuts! Oh, how we hate sugar! Why does he do this to us? (*quietly sobs*) Oh, excuse me. It's just that it's hard seeing your fellow enzymes whack out like that. Why, just last week we lost my closest friend. Albert Enzyme was trying to pull some protein out of a wad of Bubb-

licious, got stuck in it and went … you know … down the drain, flushed into oblivion. It was such a waste. And now Elaine and Ernie. They're the best little enzymes I've ever worked with.

Anyway, as I was saying, it's so exciting the way the stomach can … oh, heck, with it. No sense trying to fool you. (*pleading*) Listen to me! One of you has got to tell Joe what he's doing to us down here. We're losing enzymes and acids by the hundreds. If someone doesn't help him change his diet soon, the workers down here are going to strike. Please, talk to him. He won't listen to us, even though we make life miserable for him. Please, you gotta … (**Gut** *stops abruptly as he hears* **Amy** *and* **Andy** *screaming in the background. Two gigantic* **Tums** *enter singing, "Tum-ta-tum-tum." They attack* **Amy** *and* **Andy**.)

Andy: Gut, help us. Help us!

Amy: The Tums are neutralizing us. Help … help!

Gut: Oh, no! Hang on! Don't let it get you! (*trying in vain to get the* **Tums** *off of* **Amy** *and* **Andy. Tums** *sing "Tum-ta-tum-tum" again.*) Amy, Andy, don't die. Somebody talk to Joe!

Discussion Questions

1. Think of some of the food commercials you've seen. Besides touting nutritional value, how do advertisers motivate you to buy their product?
2. Why do you think God made us to enjoy food when too much of it or the wrong kind of it can hurt us?
3. Do you think God cares about what we eat? Why or why not?
4. Eating disorders are common among teenagers, especially girls. What do you know about bulimia or anorexia nervosa? Do you know anyone who has these problems? Why would people abuse their bodies like that?

CATERPILLAR FLIGHT

Debra J. Poling

Characters

Barry   dressed as caterpillar with feet attached down front of body and antenna on head.

Burt   same as Barry

Butterfly

Barry *and* **Burt** *are sitting on stools as if in their cocoons.*

Barry: (*yawns and stretches*) Good morning, Burt ol' boy. How'd you sleep?

Burt: (*snores*)

Barry: Burt! Burt! Wake up!

Burt: What are ya doin'?

Barry: Burt, it's morning. Time to wake up and greet the new day. (*sings*) Oh, what a beautiful morning!

Burt: Don't start singing! You remind me of my mother. She used to come into my room every day and say, (*in a high voice*) "Rise and shine, little Burtie. Oh, what a beautiful morning." I still dread waking up.

Barry: I'm sorry, Burtie, ah, I mean, Burt.

Burt: Do you know that I still have nightmares about this huge caterpillar-eating bird, who wears an apron, carries a fry pan, and sings, "Oh, what a beautiful morning," as she pushes me off my bed and out the window? I wake up in a cold sweat.

Barry: It's okay, Burt. I'll never sing again.

Burt: I'm sorry. I get carried away once in a while. I'll be fine. You know, I really like it in here. I feel so safe, so protected.

Barry: We do have nice cocoons. But I can't wait to see what happens next.

Burt: I don't want anything to happen. I'm fine just sitting here in my little cocoon being a quiet caterpillar.

Barry: How boring! Don't you want to break out of this silk ball and get some fresh air in your bones?

Burt: I don't think I have any bones. Just some flesh and guts and wiggly antennae.

Barry: Didn't you notice what someone left in our cocoons last night?

Burt: Where?

Barry: Down there!

Burt: (*picks up two sets of cardboard wings*) Well, blow me away. What are these?

Barry: They're wings, you bufflebrained bug! Didn't your mom tell you when you were a little larva about the wing fairy?

Burt: (*doubting*) The wing fairy?

Barry: Yeah. Mom told me: (*in rhyme tone*) "When you're in your cocoon, cozy and safe, the wing fairy will come and visit your place. She will leave

a gift that will let you fly, over valleys and hills and all through the sky."

Burt: That's just a fairy tale!

Barry: No, it's a fairy truth. Who else could have gotten into our cocoons?

Burt: Well, I don't believe it. And these things aren't wings. And we are caterpillars, not flies!

Barry: I know I'm not supposed to sit in here and die. We're supposed to change into something.

Burt: Impossible!

Barry: Ah ha! Directions! I knew we could find a way to get out of here.

Burt: Who put ants in your pants?!

Barry: (*looking at directions*) "Step 1: Insert tab A on wing into tab B on body." Tab B on body? Hey, Burt! Do you see a tab on me anywhere?

Burt: You're going to attach those to you? What a gross out!

Barry: What's so gross about it? When you ate that baby cockroach I never screamed, "Oh, gross me out!" even though it was the grossest gross-me-out ever.

Burt: I think it's gross. Find the stupid tab yourself.

Barry: (*looks for tab B on body, trying to attach wings to body in all the wrong places, finally holding wings to head*) Does this look right, Burt?

Burt: How would I know? I've never seen a flying caterpillar!

Barry: If only I could try flying. Then I'd know if it was right. (*bounces as if trying to fly, wings still on head*) Nuts, there's no room in here. (*moves wings to stomach*) Maybe if I put them on my stomach. (*bounces in another flying attempt*) I know. If I stand on them, they'll lift me right out of this cocoon. (*moves wings to feet and attempts to fly*)

Burt: Barry, why don't you just put the wings away and forget it? (*sarcastically*) Maybe the flying instructor fairy will come tonight and teach you how to fly in your dreams.

Barry: I hate to admit it, Burt, but you're probably right. A caterpillar can't fly. This cocoon is just to curl up and die in.

Burt: But we won't die for a while. I still feel great. Wanna play cards?

Barry: I guess.

(**Burt** *takes out cards and begins to shuffle them.* **Butterfly** *enters stage right and crosses in front of Burt and Barry.* **Barry** *sees it first.*)

Barry: Burt! Burt! Look! A flying caterpillar! I knew Mom didn't lie to me! I knew this cocoon wasn't my coffin.

Burt: A flying caterpillar! That can't be! I see it, but I don't believe it.

Barry: Burt, tab B must be on my back. Please, help me.

Burt: No way, Jose. I don't want anything to do with this. It's freaky.

Barry: Burt, it's not freaky. Ya just gotta step out and go for it. (*puts wings on himself*) See, the wings fit! I'm busting out of this cell, Bucko. Are you coming?

Burt: (*pause*) I'm comfortable here. Besides, I don't want to be laughed at for being a sissy-looking flying caterpillar. I'm staying here.

Barry: You got your wings if you change your mind. I'll be looking for you in that big blue sky. Bye, Burt. (*breaks out of his cocoon, yelling, singing, cheering as he flies offstage*)

Burt: (*picks up wings, looks in direction **Barry** flew away*) "Insert tab A on wings into Tab B on body" – gross me out!

Discussion Questions

1. What ridiculous, impossible, unrealistic dreams have you had that you'd love to come true, but that probably won't?
2. What "cocoons" – safe, secure, non-threatening places – do you like to stay in?
3. What is so hard about failing? Why do so many people give up when they try something new and it doesn't work out?
4. Why are things sometimes easier if we see that other people can do them? Why might something be *harder* after we find out someone else is also doing it?
5. What is one thing that seems too good to be true about the Christian life? (1 Cor. 2:9).

BURNING UP

Sharon Sherbondy

Characters
Mother middle-aged woman
Jim high-school senior

Scene opens with **Jim** *walking in the house feeling angry, yet controlling it. He throws his books on the floor and kicks the chair. He paces back and forth.* **Mother** *hears the noise and hurries in.*

Mother: What in the world is going on out here? Oh, it's you. For heaven's sakes, Jim, you gave me such a start.

Jim: Well, forgive me for living.

Mother: Is, uh, something wrong, dear?

Jim: No. Nothing. Why do you want to know?

Mother: Well, you just seem a little peeved about something, that's all.

Jim: Well, Mother dear, you're wrong as usual. I am not "peeved" about anything.

Mother: OK, then, how about angry, fierce, infuriated, burning, boiling mad? Am I getting close?

Jim: Why is it that you insist on making something out of nothing? I am not angry. And even if I was, I wouldn't give *him* the satisfaction of admitting it.

Mother: I see.

Jim: Good. Then maybe you'll leave me alone.

Mother: Personally, I think I'd prefer that you get it out of your system now so that I don't have to "not" hear about it all night.

Jim: I'm going to say it just one more time. I am not upset at anyone, except maybe you and your persistent nosiness! I am at all times in control of my emotions.

Mother: Really?

Jim: Let me just say, though, if — IF — I did have a dislike, a disgust, a loathing, an abhorrence for anyone, which I don't have ...

Mother: Of course not.

Jim: ... it would be towards Bob Morrison.

Mother: Why? What'd he do?

Jim: What did I just say? I said I didn't want to talk about it.

Mother: Sorry. My mistake.

Jim: You bet it is. (*pause*) Hey, what do you got the heat set on in here? 800 degrees? (*starts pulling his shirt out of his pants, unbuttoning the cuffs*)

Mother: I don't have the heat on. Maybe you're coming down with something.

Jim: I'm coming down with something, all right. (*breathing heavy*). But it's not physical. (*hitting hand in other palm*) You want to know what he did?

Mother: I'm not sure.

Jim: (*tearing his shirt open, revealing what looks like a gorilla's chest*) Man, can't we open a window or something? I'm burning up. (*slumps over slightly*)

Mother: (*soft scream*)

Jim: What? It's just an old shirt. Man, it is so hot in here. And what are you staring at?

Mother: You're so hairy ... I never noticed ...

Jim: Yeah, well, Mom, boys do grow into men, you know. I went through puberty several years ago. Can't we open a window or something? I feel like I'm breathing fire.

Mother: Well, maybe you'd be cooler if you shaved some of that off ... maybe.

Jim: I tell you, you think you know a guy. But not him. He's from a breed that should be made extinct. And boy, would I like to be the hunter that does it.

Mother: Jim, maybe it might be a good idea if you lie down and just tried to forget about what happened between you and this Bob fellow.

Jim: Mom, why don't you just stay out of things you don't know anything about? For your information, I've already forgotten about it.

Mother: Still, why don't you lie down for a while.

Jim: All right. All right. (*mumbling while he's lying down*) I'd like to make him lie down – permanently.

Mother: (*touching his forehead with her hand*) Oh my, you do feel hot! Let me get a rag to wipe your face.

Jim: Fine. Do whatever you want.

(*As* **Mother's** *talking, she's wiping* **Jim's** *face with a rag that has black cream on it. It's important that she stoop right in front of his face so that the audience can't see what's happen-*ing. *At the same time, Jim inconspicuously rubs on his hands oil that he's gotten from his mother's apron pocket.*)

Mother: Here we go – this should make you feel better. A nice cool rag is the best thing for you when you're feeling sick. That's what my mother always did for me. Now doesn't that feel better? (*lifts the rag from* **Jim's** *face and gasps*)

Jim: What's the matter now?

Mother: Your face. It's so distorted.

Jim: Thanks a lot. They say I look just like my mom.

Mother: (*backing away*) Something strange is happening here.

Jim: (*gets up and is slumped over more*) What's with you? Did Morrison get to you, too? He did, didn't he? I tell you the guy's poison.

Mother: I think things are getting out of hand here.

Jim: I gotta think. I gotta think how I'm going to get him.

(*At this point, he's rubbing his hands through his hair causing his hair to stand straight up.*) It's one thing to get to me, but now my mother. The guy is heartless. What's it going to be next, Morrison? I'll tell you what's next – it's my turn.

Mother: Oh, my goodness!

Jim: What?

Mother: Your hair!

Jim: What is your problem to-day? Maybe you should see a shrink or something. You seem to have this thing about hair lately. I'll tell you. It's enough to drive a nor-mal person mad. To see a guy like that get away with murder. Murder. Yeah. I like that word. Yeah. Why, just the thought of it makes me thirsty. Mom, we got any blood in the house? Some of Morrison's would really quench my thirst.

Mother: Ahhhhh. Uh, Jim, dear, don't you think maybe you're making too much of this thing with Bob? What could he have possibly done to make you hate him so?

Jim: So … *SO*, you're on his side. I should have known. My own mother. My own flesh and blood turning against me – the whole world out to get me – all because of Bob Morrison. Well, it's lucky for you, for everyone, that I don't let things get to me. I may hate the guy, but at least I don't get ugly about it.

Discussion Questions

1. What makes you angry?
2. How do you express your anger?
3. How do you handle other people's anger?
4. How do people sin in anger? (Eph. 4:26).
5. What guidelines does the Bible give us for expressing our anger? (Eph. 4:26, Matt. 18:15).

THE EXCHANGE-AN-IDENTITY SHOP

Debra J. Poling

Characters

Joy	sixteen-year-old high school student, gutsy, likes to experiment
Brian	seventeen-year-old high school student, skeptical, likes Joy
Rob	Twilight Zone type, owner of the shop
Suzy Socialite	bubbly, spacey, as her name implies
Stacy Submissive	very attractive, submissive, servant type to a fault
Neil No-Brain	alcoholic, drug-addict type
Stephanie Spiritual	no brain, just plastic smile

In the Exchange-an-Identity Shop, the various "identities" are scattered throughout the shop, standing with their backs to the audience. **Rob** *is standing back to audience beside a desk on which are the request forms for exchanging identities.* **Brian** *and* **Joy** *enter through door on stage left. (Creative costuming will give this an extra visual impact.)*

Joy: Come on, Brian. I don't understand why you aren't more excited about coming here today.

Brian: Well, I just think there are more romantic places to go on a date than to a store that sells personalities.

Joy: I told you a hundred times, you don't buy personalities here, you exchange them.

Brian: Whatever. It's still not a place I picture Tom Cruise taking his date.

Joy: (*playing up to him*) Brian, Honey, this is only the beginning of our date ... just be patient.

Brian: (*lighting up*) Yeah, Joy?

Joy: Yeah ... now let's go in.

Brian: Whatever you say, Babe! (**Joy** and **Brian** enter and notice all the mannequins standing around.) Man, this place is crowded.

Joy: Sure is ... (noticing the silence). Brian, no one's talking ... or moving.

Brian: There's something strange going on here ...

Joy: Yeah, let's go.

Rob: (Just as they are getting ready to go, one of the mannequins turns around – it's **Rob**, the owner.) May I help you?

**Brian &
Joy:** (scream. **Joy** jumps into **Brian's** arms.)

Brian: Who are you?

Rob: I am Rob, the owner of the Exchange-an-Identity Shop. I assume you want to change your identity?

Joy: Well, we are interested in ...

Brian: (trying to shut her up) Ah, I think these other people were before us, and seeing as we don't have all day, we'll just come back another time. Thank you. (grabbing **Joy**) Bye-bye. (goes to door. It's locked.) The door is locked. Could you open it?

Rob: Yes.

Brian: Good. (waits, but **Rob** just stands there smiling) Ah, would you open it?

Rob: No.

Brian: I didn't think you would. (trying to stay calm and collected) Well, we'll just have a seat until you finish with the others. (**Brian** and **Joy** sit down.)

Rob: I believe you're next.

Joy: What about all these other people?

Rob: They're not customers. They're our display models.

Joy: Oh, that's why they aren't talking...they're dummies!

Rob: I wouldn't say that too loudly.

Joy: I have to admit, I was pretty scared. But now this seems like it's going to be lots of fun, right Brian?

Brian: (*still skeptical*) Why is the door locked?

Rob: It's not locked, it just sticks. Go ahead and try it.

Joy: Brian, stop worrying. (*to* **Rob**) Now, why don't you show us what you've got. (**All three** *walk over to* **Suzy Socialite. Brian** *lags behind a bit and tries the door. It opens.*)

Rob: Joy ... that is your name, isn't it?

Joy: Why, yes.

Rob: I thought we'd look at this model first, because I perceive a spirit in you that loves people and fun. This is Model #2324 – Suzy Socialite.

Joy: Hey, Brian, look at this!

She looks just like that cheerleader from Jefferson High who moved away last month.

Brian: Yeah, she does.

Rob: We try to pattern our models after average, everyday people. Let me activate her for you.

Suzy: Hi, I'm Suzy. Life is just so wonderful, isn't it? And you're just wonderful, aren't you? I think the highest call of a high-school student is to learn all the cheers one can and be able to recite them while smiling and doing cartwheels. I know all the football players' measurements and the entire basketball team's phone numbers. I read all the latest magazines and spend hours watching ... (**Rob** *deactivates her.*)

Rob: What do you think? This is one of our most in-demand identities. Everyone wants to be popular, right Joy?

Brian: This is the most idiotic thing I've ever seen. Joy, let's get out of here.

Rob: How terribly rude of me. I forgot all about you, Brian. I think I have just the thing you need. Walk this way, please (**Brian** *and* **Joy** *follow* **Rob,** *imitating his walk*). Brian, this is Model #2301. Stacy, say hello to Brian.

Stacy: Hello, Brian. Can I get anything for you? Some tea perhaps, or maybe me?

Brian: You?

Stacy: Why, yes. I am Stacy Submissive and I will do anything you want. You have a spot on your shirt. Let me wash it for you. (*She begins to pull off* **Brian's** *shirt.*)

Brian: Leave my shirt alone.

Stacy: Oh dear, your shoe's untied. Here, let me ... (*ties* **Brian's** *shoe*)

Brian: I can tie my own shoe, thank you.

Stacy: You seem so tense. Perhaps a back rub would help. (*rubs* **Brian's** *back*)

Brian: I don't need ... (*he begins to enjoy it*) a ... back ... rub ... ah, up a bit higher, to the right ... (*coming to his senses*) Wait a minute. *I* don't want to be like that!

Rob: (*aside, to* **Brian**) I know, but perhaps you could convince Joy to give her ...

Joy: (*looking at another mannequin*) Rob, what kind of identity is this?

Rob: This is Model #3331, Neil No-Brain. This is what we call our economy model. It's for people who don't have much to trade in, but are still looking for an identity with a little life to it. The only drawback is that you have to fuel it up before it'll run. We have found that a shot or two of ninety-proof helps it run at peak performance.

Neil: (**Rob** *pours a shot of alcohol into* **Neil No-Brain**. *Slowly* **Neil** *comes to life.*) Oh, wow! Oh, wow!

Brian: Looks like he's warming up.

Neil: (*full of life*) OH, WOW! OH, WOW!

Joy: Looks like he's warmed up.

Neil: (*slowing down*) Oh, wow! Oh, wow!

Rob: Yeah, he's slowing down now. (**Neil** *shuts down.*)

Brian and Joy: (*reacting to how strange* **Neil** *was*) Oh, wow!

Rob: Many people your age find this model a fun way to get rid of pressure and fit right in with the crowd. Well, now that you've had a chance to look at some of our models, let me get the proper forms so you can get the identity of your dreams.

Brian: Wait a minute. I'm not giving up my identity. I kinda like who I am.

Joy: Brian, you are so weird. Nobody likes themselves. And even if they did, nobody else would like them. Come on, it'll be fun.

Brian: Joy, you're nuts! I may not have the identity of my dreams, but this is what God gave me, and I'm staying the way I am.

Rob: Did I hear you say "God"? This model should suit you just fine. This is #3444 – Stephanie Spiritual. (**Rob** *activates* **Stephanie**.)

Stephanie: (*stands there with a big smile on her face*)

Brian: But she's not saying anything.

Rob: Of course, everyone knows that religious people have *no personality*!

Brian: That's not true.

Joy: (*apologetically*) Brian really believes God has big plans for his future.

Brian: I've seen enough!

Rob: Oh, so you've made your choice?

Brian: Yeah, I've made my choice, and my choice is to leave. Come on, Joy.

Joy: I'm not sure I want to leave yet.

Brian: You're not seriously considering giving up your identity for one of these, are you?

Joy: Well, I think it might be fun to be popular, like Suzy Socialite.

Brian: You're going to give up all you are for someone as shallow as that?

Joy: Get real, Brian. You know I could never win a popularity contest, and neither could you. It wouldn't hurt for you to have a better personality.

Brian: I may not be God's gift to the senior class, but I am unique and I'm not trading in what God gave me on a new model. (*exits*)

Joy: Brian, wait ... don't get so upset ...

Rob: Don't worry about him. He'll come to his senses when he sees what a difference a new identity will do for you.

Joy: I suppose.

Rob: Shall we get to work? Why don't you just take these forms with you and we'll get started. You wanted Model #2324, right?

Joy: (*reading the forms*) Ah, right. (*as they exit*) What's this about no refunds or exchanges allowed?

Discussion Questions

1. If you could be anyone, whom would you most want to be? Why?
2. What do you want to change about yourself?
3. Name two things you really like about yourself.
4. The Bible says we are made in the

image of God (Gen. 1:26-27). What do you think that means?

5. Ephesians 5:1 says, "Be imitators of God, therefore, as dearly loved children and live a life of love, just as Christ loved us and gave himself up for us" What are some ways you can imitate God in your life and in how you feel about yourself?

Dating

JUST A LITTLE COVER-UP

Debra J. Poling

Characters

Tiffany	seventeen years old, real together physically, knows how to get her man, dressed to kill
Joan	seventeen years old, normal looking, sharp, but not sexy … yet! Wears normal glasses and robe
Sean	Tiffany's date, seventeen years old, a real "dude" to the max
Brian	seventeen years old, Joan's blind date

Opens with **Tiffany** *and* **Joan** *in Tiffany's bedroom getting ready for dates with Sean and Brian.* **Tiffany** *is leaning over* **Joan**, *who is sitting at a vanity table looking straight into audience through an imaginary mirror. When dates arrive, scene moves to living room where there are two chairs and a doorway leading outside.*

Tiffany: Just a little more cover-up and he'll never know you're hiding a zit.

Joan: Go easy, Tiff. I want him to know there's a face behind all this.

Tiffany: Don't worry. You look awesome. Now let's see what we can do with this hair. (*begins to brush it*)

Joan: Tiffany, are you sure you don't know anything about this guy?

Tiffany: All I know is that Sean asked me out and needed someone to double with his friend. So I said I'd come up with someone.

Joan: I don't know why I ever let you talk me into this. What if the guy's a nerd? Ow! Don't pull so hard.

Tiffany: He's Sean's friend, and Sean doesn't hang around with geeks.

Joan: You never know. You sometimes hang around with me … and I'm not your type.

Tiffany: Yeah, but I look at you as sort of a challenge. I figure, here's a girl who's never dated, who's basically pretty sharp and just needs a bit of work on her appearance. And since I know about looking totally awesome, I figured I'd take you on as a challenge.

Joan: (*less than enthusiastically*) How generous of you.

Tiffany: (*She has finished fixing Joan's hair into a sexy style.*) There, what do you think?

Joan: I think I look ridiculous. I would never wear my hair this way!

Tiffany: That's precisely what I'm working on! Now get your dress on.

Joan: Aw, Tiff, I just don't know if I can go …

Tiffany: Hurry up, they'll be here soon. (**Joan** *leaves for a quick change. She has dress on under robe and changes offstage.*) You know, Joan, I've been thinking about your name. Joan is such a boring name. Maybe we should change it to something more appealing, like Susie or Tricia or … Courtney. That's it! When the guys come I'm going to introduce you as Courtney. They'll never know!

Joan: (*entering in a dull, loose fitting, elastic neck dress, and low heels*) I'm not going to change my name! Tiffany, I can't change everything just for some guy I don't even know!

Tiffany: (*noticing her dress*) Joan, you're not serious about that dress, are you?

Joan: What's wrong with it?

Tiffany: It's so ... so ... loose!

Joan: You always said this was cute.

Tiffany: Cute, maybe ... but not for a date! Did you bring anything else?

Joan: No.

Tiffany: (*puts a wide belt on* **Joan**, *hikes the skirt up a bit so it's more of a mini, and drops the neckline off the shoulders as she's talking*) Well, maybe if we put a belt on it, raise the skirt up a bit, and bare your shoulders ... now, let's see how you look.

Joan: Tiff, I can't breathe! You've got the belt too tight.

Tiffany: Don't loosen it. You look awesome. Turn around once. Let me get a good look at you.

Joan: (*turning hesitantly*) This is nuts.

Tiffany: Now then, there's just one more thing. (*holding up two wads of Kleenex*) Put these on.

Joan: What are these for?

Tiffany: To help ... you know ... fill you out a bit!

Joan: I will not! (*throws the Kleenex on the floor*)

Tiffany: Oh, all right ... skip the Kleenex. But you've got to leave the glasses behind! (*takes them off* **Joan**) You know, you don't look half bad. I bet your date won't be able to keep his hands off.

Joan: Wait a minute! What's expected of me on this date?

Tiffany: You mean, as in sex?

Joan: Yeah!

Tiffany: Honey, the idea is to tease, not give. (*doorbell rings*) They're here! Come on. Now remember, your name is Courtney. (**Tiffany** *drags* **Joan** *to the front door through the living room*)

Joan: Tiffany, I told you …

Tiffany: (*smiling and opening the door*) Hi Sean, we've been waiting for you.

Sean: Hi, Tiffany. You look ravishing! (*They are both playing up to each other.*)

Brian: (*clears his throat*)

Sean: Oh … ah, Tiff, this is Brian.

Tiffany: Hi there … oh, and this is Courtney.

Joan: Tiff …

Brian: (*entering the living room and moving in on* **Joan**, *taking her hand to kiss it*) The pleasure is mine. (**Joan** *pulls it away.*)

Joan: (*shocked*) Hello, Brian. Tiff, I need to see you a minute! (*pulling* **Tiffany** *to another corner of the living room.* **Sean** *and* **Brian** *get together and talk between themselves.*)

Tiffany: What's wrong?

Joan: I know my blind date!

Tiffany: Hey, that's great!

Joan: No, it's not. He's my lab partner. I sit next to him every day.

Tiffany: So?

Joan: So! He doesn't recognize me … yet. He knows my name isn't Courtney.

Tiffany: Well, play along until he figures it out. It'll be fun. And relax, you're too tense. (*returning to the* **guys**, *with* **Joan** *reluctantly following*) Sorry for the delay … a little girl talk. Well, why don't we sit down for a minute? (*Since* *there are only two chairs in the room,* **Tiff** *sits on* **Sean's** *lap, and* **Brian** *signals* **Joan** *to sit on his)*

Joan: I don't feel like sitting.

Brian: Aw, come on. (*pulls* **Joan** *onto his lap*)

Joan: (*gasping for air*) I can't breathe … I can't breathe!

Brian: (*getting a little freaked out, lets her go*) What's wrong?

Joan: (*catching her breath*) My belt's too tight.

Brian: You know something, Courtney, you seem vaguely familiar to me.

Tiffany: Nonsense. Brian, don't you think you'd remember if you saw someone as awesome as Courtney before?

Brian: (*warming up to* **Joan** *again*) I sure would. I think it's your voice that seems familiar to me.

Joan: (*in a high pitched voice*) How silly!

Sean: Well, we've got all night to figure out where Brian has seen Courtney before. Let's get going.

Tiffany: Where are we going tonight?

Sean: Well, since you two look ready for action, I thought we'd go for a little ride under the moonlight to some quiet spot and … get to know each other better.

Joan: (*breaking down*) That's it … I can't keep this up any longer. Tiff, this just isn't me.

Brian: Now I know where I've heard that voice before – you're my lab partner! But I thought your name was Jean or June or something like that.

Joan: Joan. I'm surprised you knew even that much.

Brian: But you look so different … so … good.

Joan: You can thank Tiffany for that. (*getting a bit mad*) You know, Brian, I'm surprised you even recognized my

Brian: voice. The only time you talk to me is to get answers for exams.

Brian: I guess I never noticed what was hidden under those glasses.

Joan: Now you're seeing me hiding under a lot of makeup and sexy clothes.

Brian: And I like what I see!

Joan: Well, I don't. And I don't like the change I see in you just because I look this way. This isn't me! I may not be the most attractive hunk of flesh you ever set your eyes on, but I am intelligent, and I can be fun to be around. Now, if you'll excuse me. I'd like to get out of these clothes, wash my face, and put my glasses on. I can't see a thing! (*exits*)

(**All** *stand there dumbfounded for a moment*)

Sean: Well, you win some, you lose some. Let's go, Brian, we'll find someone on the streets for you.

Brian: (*still taken aback*) I think I'll wait here for Joan.

Tiffany: Come on, Brian. She's not going to be any fun. I tried, but she's just too beige, like totally boring.

Brian: I said I'm going to wait for her.

Sean: Okay, okay. See you around. (**Sean** *and* **Tiff** *exit*)

(**Brian** *paces for a moment, then sits in a chair, thinking very deeply about what has just happened. Lights fade slowly.*)

Discussion Questions

1. What's one of the dumbest things you've done to get someone to notice you?
2. What qualities do you look for in someone of the opposite sex? Do you think most people are looking for those same characteristics?
3. Is it realistic to think we should *never* be concerned with how someone else looks when we pick friends or consider who to date? How do you handle the problem of wanting to be with people who look nice while also trying to find "hidden" qualities in a person?
4. Why do you think people some-

times go to great lengths to be different than they really are? What could you tell someone who said they didn't like themselves as they really were? (1 Sam. 16:7).

A DIME A DOZEN

Sharon Sherbondy

Characters
Polly   freshman girl
Richard   cocky senior guy

Scene opens with **Polly** *talking on the phone in her living room.*

Polly: Sally, I'm so excited I can hardly stand it! I've been to the bathroom five times in the last half hour. I've washed off and put on my makeup three times … because I want to look perfect. I've gargled almost a full bottle of mouthwash plus went and bought some Close-Up toothpaste. If my breath doesn't magnetize him, nothing will.

What do you mean, taking this a little far? Do you know how long I have been in love with Richard Noffzinger? He's gorgeous, he's tough, he's popular, to say the least. Okay, and a little vain. And to think that he actually asked me out. I could faint every time I think about it.

Well, what about Harvey? Harvey, schmarvey, the kid will get over me. I've gotten over him. Sally, guys like Harvey are a dime a dozen. Richard Noffzingers come along once in a lifetime, and this is one girl who's not going to pass him up. *(doorbell)* Oh my gosh, the doorbell! He's here. What am I going to say? How should I act when I open the door? Oh, man, I gotta go to the bathroom again! *(doorbell)* Oh, no, he rang it again. All right, I'll go answer it. Sally, this girl is about to cross over into womanhood. I'll call you the moment he tears himself away from me. Okay. Bye. *(doorbell)* I'm coming. *(fixes her hair, smells her armpits and breath, straightens her clothes, walks to the door, and takes a deep breath.*

Opens door) Hi.

Richard: (*struts in*) Hey, Polly, looking good tonight. (*struts over to the couch and sits down.* **Polly** *stands there staring.*) Well, hey, baby, you gonna stand there all night or are you gonna come here and be with the one you adore?

Polly: Oh, sure. (*sits on couch next to* **Richard**)

Richard: So what do you got to eat around here?

Polly: Eat? Oh, I thought we were going out.

Richard: Hey, I don't spend money on a girl on the first date. I gotta find out if she's worth it first. (*gives her a squeeze*)

Polly: Well, that's certainly … wise, I guess. Well, uh, we've got pizza or hamburgers or …

Richard: Got any beer?

Polly: Beer? No, my parents don't drink.

Richard: You should have told me. I would have brought my own.

Polly: Oh, I don't think my parents would like that very much.

Richard: Let me get this straight. Am I dating you or your parents?

Polly: (*with reluctance*) Good point.

Richard: So, what'd you think of the big game last Friday? Am I or am I not the best darn quarterback this school has ever had?

Polly: Yeah. You were pretty good.

Richard: Pretty good?! I'd say more like fantastic, incredible, unbelievable. Listen, baby, I am star material. So why don't you stick to things you know something about (*softens*) like, uh, good-looking guys. (*looks himself over*) Yeah, looks like mine don't come your way every day, do they? Some guys gotta work to look like this;

others are just naturally blessed. Take you, for instance. On a scale from one to ten, I'd give you a ... stand up and turn around.

Polly: What?

Richard: Stand up and turn around.

Polly: *(embarrassed)* Come on, cut it out.

Richard: I mean it. I want to be able to get a full view so I can score you fairly. So stand up.

Polly: Oh, all right.

Richard: Turn around.

Polly: *(turns around)* I feel so silly.

Richard: Hmmm. Not bad. The man likes what he sees. But, you know, it would be a lot easier to score you if you'd take a few layers off, if you know what I mean.

Polly: Richard!

Richard: Come on, Polly. Don't play Miss Innocence with me. I know you too well. You girls are all alike. You lead a guy on, tease him every chance you get, practically throw yourself at his feet, but then when he gives you what you've been asking for you get all upset, like you can't believe what's happening. Tell me, do your mothers teach you these games or is it something you're born with?

Polly: *(getting a little angry)* I have not been teasing you or throwing myself at your feet.

Richard: No?

Polly: No.

Richard: Okay. We'll play it your way. Just settle down. So, hey, what's a guy gotta do around here to get something to eat, get it himself?

Polly: Sure, if you want. Help yourself.

Richard: That's cute, doll, but that's what you're here for – to bring me my food, open my beer, rub my back, keep me warm. (**Polly's** *getting* _furious_) And, uh, speaking of keeping me warm, why don't we turn up the temperature in here a little. What do you say? (_makes his move_)

Polly: Richard, let me go.

Richard: Come on. Let's can the games. I know what you want, baby.

Polly: Richard, please.

Richard: Oooo, I love it when you beg.

Polly: Richard, I mean it. Leave me alone!

Richard: Polly, relax. Come on, don't let me down. I've got too much resting on this.

Polly: What's that supposed to mean?

Richard: Oh, nothing, just a little wager I've got going with a couple guys, that's all.

Polly: What kind of little wager? No, really, I'm interested. I just want to know what's expected of me.

Richard: That a girl! Well, some of the guys said you'd probably be a real loser when it came to, you know, but I told them that it just took the right man to turn you into putty.

Polly: Hmmm. How right you are. (_seductively_) And you know, I've got just the thing to make this into an even more surprising evening for you, but you've got to close your eyes first.

Richard: Yeah? What is it?

Polly: It's this. (_picks up book and slams it on top of **Richard's** head as hard as she can_)

Richard: Hey, what the heck?

Polly: That's what I think of you and your gambling buddies! (_hits **Richard** again_)

Richard: Hey, will you knock it off?

Polly: (_hits **Richard** again_) And that's what I think of you and your oversized ego!

Richard: Polly, I'm warning you.

Polly: (_hits **Richard** towards the_

door) And this is what I think of you!

Richard: What? Are you crazy? Are you nuts?

Polly: Yeah, I'm crazy! I am nuts for ever thinking that I was the least bit interested in you, that you were the guy of my dreams. And I'm crazy for cancelling a date with Harvey, just to be used and abused by you.

Richard: You are whacked out, you know that? You don't know what you're passing up.

Polly: And you're going to be maimed for life if you don't get out of here right now. (*starts hitting* **Richard** *again*)

(**Richard** *is yelling while he's running out.* **Polly** *stands at the door furious, al-most physically shaking, trying to pull herself together. She slowly turns, walks over, and sits down by the phone. She picks it up and dials.*)

Hello, Sally? It's me. Yeah, he's gone already. How was it? Let me put it this way. I'm calling Harvey tonight to apologize. Because I've discovered that Harveys come along once in a lifetime, and it's the Richard Noffzingers that are a dime a dozen.

Discussion Questions
1. How would most girls respond to Richard?
2. What would you have done if you were Polly?
3. What advice would you have given Polly if you were Sally?
4. What qualities do you look for in a date?
5. How do you feel about 2 Corinthians 6:14?

TO LEAP OR NOT TO LEAP

Debra J. Poling

Characters

Paul   high-school junior
Judy   high-school junior
Judy's Thoughts   offstage voice
Paul's Thoughts   offstage voice

Scene opens with **Paul** *and* **Judy** *in a car. Paul is driving.* **Judy's Thoughts** *and* **Paul's Thoughts** *are voices offstage. When the Thoughts are talking, Paul and Judy should act like they are thinking and responding to their own thoughts. The closer the Thought voices are to Paul and Judy's the better the effect.*

Paul: Well, did you like the movie?

Judy: It was okay.

Paul: I hope those gory scenes didn't frighten you too much.

Judy: Oh, no.

Judy's Thoughts: You planned it out so that those gory parts would get me scared and I'd hide my face in your shoulder.

Paul's Thoughts: That gory stuff worked better than the guys said it would. She couldn't get close enough to her big, strong, protective man.

Paul: Do you want something to eat?

Judy: Do you?

Paul: If you do.

Judy's Thoughts: Let's see. The movie was four dollars each, and food will probably be another seven dollars. I don't want him to go broke on the first date.

Paul's Thoughts: Please, please don't be hungry. I don't have any more money!

Judy's Thoughts: Rule number one – make him think you eat like a bird. It's the feminine thing to do.

Judy: No, Paul, I really don't want anything to eat.

Paul's Thoughts: (*huge sigh of relief*)

Paul: Are you sure?

Paul's Thoughts: You idiot, don't push her!

Judy: I'm sure.

Paul: Well, where to next?

Judy: What time is it?

Paul's Thoughts: Nuts, it's ten-thirty already. She has to be home by eleven.

Paul: It's ten-thirty.

Judy: I suppose I should be getting home, unless you have a better idea.

Paul's Thoughts: Boy, have I got a better idea!

Paul: We could just drive around a bit.

Judy: Okay. But I need to be home in half an hour.

Paul's Thoughts: Half an hour, half an hour. Ten minutes to get to Lover's Leap, ten minutes to get her home, that leaves ten minutes on the leap.

Judy's Thoughts: I hope he doesn't go to Lover's Leap. All the girls will ask, "Did he take you to Lover's Leap? Did he try anything? Did you let him? Judy, girls who want to be asked out again have to give a little!" If he doesn't go, then I can just say he didn't give me a chance. He can be the "straight" one.

Paul's Thoughts: Here we go a-leaping! Wait until the guys hear this. "First base?" they'll ask. "No," I'll say. "Second base?" they'll ask.

The People Who Brought You This Book...

─ **invite you to discover MORE valuable youth-ministry resources.** ─

Youth Specialties offers an assortment of books, publications, tapes, and events, all designed to encourage and train youth workers and their kids. Just return this card, and we'll send you FREE information on our products and services.

Please send me the FREE Youth Specialties Catalog and information on upcoming Youth Specialties events.

Are you: ☐ An adult youth worker   ☐ A youth

Name _____

Church/Org. _____

Address _____

City_____ State _____ Zip _____

Phone Number (_____) _____

The People Who Brought You This Book...

─ **invite you to discover MORE valuable youth-ministry resources.** ─

Youth Specialties offers an assortment of books, publications, tapes, and events, all designed to encourage and train youth workers and their kids. Just return this card, and we'll send you FREE information on our products and services.

Please send me the FREE Youth Specialties Catalog and information on upcoming Youth Specialties events.

Are you: ☐ An adult youth worker   ☐ A youth

Name _____

Church/Org. _____

Address _____

City_____ State _____ Zip _____

Phone Number (_____) _____

Call toll-free to order:

(800) 776-8008

BUSINESS REPLY MAIL
FIRST CLASS   PERMIT NO. 16   EL CAJON, CA

POSTAGE WILL BE PAID BY ADDRESSEE

YOUTH SPECIALTIES
1224 Greenfield Dr.
El Cajon, CA 92021-9989

Call toll-free to order:

(800) 776-8008

NO POSTAGE
NECESSARY
IF MAILED
IN THE
UNITED STATES

BUSINESS REPLY MAIL
FIRST CLASS   PERMIT NO. 16   EL CAJON, CA

POSTAGE WILL BE PAID BY ADDRESSEE

YOUTH SPECIALTIES
1224 Greenfield Dr.
El Cajon, CA 92021-9989

"Keep going," I'll say. "Third base?" "Getting closer." "Home run?" "Yeah," I'll say.

Paul: *Home run!*

Judy: What did you say?

Paul: Ah ... nothing. I was just thinking about baseball.

Judy: Oh.

Judy's Thoughts: Good, he's not thinking about Lover's Leap.

Paul's Thoughts: Home run? What am I thinking? I could ruin our friendship by trying to do what the guys want to hear. And what business is it of theirs? I had a good time with Judy. And everybody knows what the leap does to friendships.

Paul: (*turning the car around*) Judy, I think it's time I get you home.

Judy: So soon?

Paul: Yeah.

Judy & Paul: There's something I want to tell you.

Paul: You go first.

Judy: No, you go first.

Paul: Judy, I had a good time with you tonight. And, well, I was just thinking about taking you to Lover's Leap. And I decided I don't want to go there with you.

Judy: Don't you like me?

Paul: Yes, I like you. That's just the point.

Judy: I see, you like me, and the way you show it is by taking me home.

Paul: Yeah, I don't want to be with you.

Judy: (*upset*) You don't want to be with me?

Paul: Wait, you don't understand. I want to be with you. But not at Lover's Leap. The reason I was taking you there is so that

I could impress my friends.

Judy: I wanted to tell you I was thinking the same thing. My friends say that unless I give a little, you won't ask me out again.

Paul: Can I ask you a very personal question?

Judy: I guess.

Paul: Have you ever given a little and felt good about it?

Judy: No. I've done some pretty stupid things hoping to get asked out again.

Paul: I've blown it a few times on dates, too.

Judy: (*pauses to think*) Paul, how come you decided not to take me to the Leap when you've always gone before?

Paul: I like you. I don't want to risk hurting you just to impress my friends.

Judy: Thanks. But what do we tell our friends now?

Paul: We'll just tell them we didn't go to Lover's Leap and that we had a good time and that we are going out again.

Judy: We are?

Paul: Yeah ... I mean, is that okay?

Judy: I'd be happy to go out with you. Thanks for being so honest with me. And Paul, I have to admit I wasn't honest with you before.

Paul: Oh?

Judy: Yeah. I really am hungry. Can we get something to eat?

Paul: Ah ... no. I don't have any more money.

Judy: But what would you have done if I said I was hungry before?

Paul: I could have always robbed a 7-Eleven!

Discussion Questions

1. Do you think most people who get involved sexually do it because of peer pressure or because they like the feelings? What other reasons might two people have for becoming sexually active in their relationship?

2. What are some of the best reasons you know of for keeping sex only in marriage? Are these realistic in today's sex-crazed society?

3. Why do you think God made sex?

4. If it feels good and it's God's idea anyway, why shouldn't everybody enjoy sex whenever they want to? (1 Thess. 4:3)

5. What are some fun and creative ways two people can show they like each other without having sex?

GOING NOWHERE

Sharon Sherbondy

Characters

Jim average seventeen-year-old
Sandy average seventeen-year-old, dressed a little seductively
Mary average seventeen-year-old, dressed more conservatively
Bill average seventeen-year-old

Stage is set with table and four chairs at a restaurant. **Jim**, **Sandy, Bill,** *and* **Mary** *are sitting at the table.*

Jim: When are you going to grow up? (*blows through his straw at passerby*)

Sandy: Me grow up? You're the one acting like a two-year-old, spitting water at everyone that walks by.

Jim: So why don't you get up and leave? Then I can spit water at you, too.

Sandy: Very funny. Come on, Mary. You want to go to the bathroom with me?

Mary: Sure.

Jim: Aren't you a big enough girl to go by yourself? What are you going to do in there, anyway?

Sandy: None of your business.

(**Girls** *walk to stage right.* **Guys** *freeze.* **Girls** *pantomime being at the mirror in a bathroom.*)

Sandy: Sometimes I could just scream, he makes me so mad! No, not sometimes, all the time. One of these days I'm going to just drop him like a hot potato. Then we'll see who gets the last laugh.

Mary: Sandy, you're always talking about dumping him but you never do.

Sandy: Well, you just wait. One of these days I'm going to …

Mary: One of these days, nothing. Why don't you just stop talking and do it? I'm sick of listening to you constantly crying about how rotten Jim is. If you're so unhappy with him, then why don't you just break up with him?

Sandy: Yeah, sure, and where would that leave me?

Mary: It would leave you free to do what you want, see who you want, be with your friends more.

Sandy: Mary, I don't have any friends except for Jim.

Mary: You've got me, and I know Linda and Sue and Karen …

Sandy: Mary, I quit hanging around with them a long time ago when I started dating Jim. I don't think they'd be too thrilled to have me suddenly reappear, just because I'm not dating him anymore.

Mary: How do you know until you try?

Sandy: Besides, I can't talk to girls. I don't have anything in common with them.

Mary: Sandy, come on.

Sandy: I'm serious. I've just always

been able to talk to guys better.

Mary: You call what you do with Jim talking and getting along?

Sandy: Mary, you just don't understand our relationship. And whether you want to believe me or not, I just get along better with guys than I do with girls. (**Girls** *freeze*)

(**Guys** *unfreeze*)

Bill: Man, you and Sandy sure fight a lot.

Jim: That was nothing! You should see us when we really go at it.

Bill: What do you fight about?

Jim: Who knows? Nothing and everything. She's just a pain in the butt most of the time.

Bill: So why do you keep going out with her?

Jim: We've been dating for two years. I guess you could say she's like a bad habit.

Bill: So why don't you break the habit?

Jim: Yeah, I've thought about it, but I don't know. It would be more work to start dating somebody new than it would be to keep putting up with her.

Bill: What about not dating at all?

Jim: Yeah, right.

Bill: I'm serious.

Jim: So am I.

Bill: All right. Be miserable. See if I care.

Jim: Listen, Bill, if I dropped Sandy, I don't even want to think about what kinds of things she'd say about me. And then if I didn't date anyone after her? Everyone would think I was, you know.

Bill: I don't know why I try to talk to you.

Jim: Okay, okay. I'll admit, it's just easier to stick with a bad habit than it is to start a good one. (**Guys** *freeze*)

(**Girls** *unfreeze*)

Sandy: Mary, listen. I'm glad you care. It means a lot to me. Really. But it's just that I'm different than you. You're, I don't know, more independent. I need a guy.

Mary: Sandy, that's not true. No girl *needs* a guy.

Sandy: Well, I do. I couldn't stand not having a guy around.

Mary: Even a guy as lousy as Jim?

Sandy: He's not lousy.

Mary: What do you mean? I'm just repeating what you always say about him.

Sandy: That's different. No matter what you think of Jim, he's still a lot better than no guy at all. (*pause*) Oh, what's the use? See why I said I can't talk to girls? (**Girls** *freeze*)

(**Guys** *unfreeze*)

Jim: All right, I'll admit that probably the reason I keep going out with Sandy is that it's more convenient. She's always there. I never have to worry about not having a date or going someplace alone.

Bill: Sounds real meaningful.

Jim: Hey, do you hear me complaining?

Bill: Yeah, well, what *else* is convenient about her?

Jim: (*smiles*) Hey, it's not like I'm pushing her into anything. She's told me it helps her to feel secure. And who am I to deny a girl security, huh?

Bill: (*sarcastically*) Sounds like real love to me.

Jim: It's probably as close as we'll ever get to it, and it'll do for now.

Bill: How convenient. (**Guys** *freeze*)

(**Girls** *unfreeze*)

Sandy: Listen, Mary, don't give me that holier-than-thou look. If you had parents like mine, you'd be the same way.

Mary: What have your parents got to do with anything?

Sandy: If they'd given me the love I needed …

Mary: Oh, Sandy, come on.

Sandy: Well, it's the truth. Until Jim came along I was really unhappy.

Mary: You call this happiness?

Sandy: Look, if you were me you'd do the same thing. (**Girls** *freeze*)

(**Guys** *unfreeze*)

Jim: You know what I really like about Sandy?

Bill: I'm afraid to ask.

Jim: Her parents. No, really. They're neat people. I guess I keep hoping that maybe a little of them will rub off on her.

Bill: How long are you going to keep waiting?

Jim: I don't know.

Bill: Sounds like a wasted life to me.

Jim: If you were me, you'd do the same thing. (**Guys** *freeze*)

(**Girls** *unfreeze*)

Sandy: Hey, come on, what are we doing? We're beginning to sound like Jim and me, fighting over nothing. You live your life and I'll live mine. Okay?

Mary: Sure.

Sandy: All right. Maybe I should break up with Jim, but I can't. Maybe someday, but not now. (**Girls** *head back to table*)

(**Guys** *unfreeze*)

Jim: We've broken up thousands of times, you know. But somehow we always end up back together. Hey, it'll all work out.

Sandy: Well, we're back. Hey, who drank the rest of my pop?

Jim: I did. You were in the stupid bathroom so long I thought you weren't coming back.

Sandy: You're a real nice guy, you know that?

Jim: So what do you want to do now? Not that there's a whole lot of choice since you spent the night in the john.

Sandy: If you say that one more time …

Mary: Uh, I think I'm going home.

Bill: Me, too.

Jim: Just when things are warming up?

Mary: I'll call you.

Sandy: Okay.

Bill: Catch you later. (**Mary** *and* **Bill** *exit.*)

Jim: (*pause*) Well, now what do you want to do?

Sandy: I don't know.

Jim: My parents aren't home.

Sandy: Sure, why not?

Discussion Questions

1. What are Jim and Sandy really afraid of?
2. If you or someone you know is like Sandy or Jim, what can be done to help build your or their self-esteem so a date isn't needed?
3. What's it feel like not to date?
4. What's it feel like to be stuck with a date?

TURN AROUND IS FAIR PLAY

Sharon Sherbondy

Characters

Craig clean-cut high-school senior
Sherry attractive high-school senior
Jack casual looking, laid-back high-school senior
Kelly average high-school sopho-more
Waitress waitresses at a hamburger joint

The song, "Honesty," by Billy Joel is used in this sketch.

Scene I: *Stage is set with door frame and two chairs in the center. Dim lighting throughout. **Sherry** is standing in darkened area. **Craig** walks up and knocks at her door.*

Sherry: (*talking to someone off-stage*) No, don't fix me anything to drink. I'll get something at the show. (*opens door and is surprised*) Oh, Craig, hi. Uhm, what a surprise. Our date's not tonight, is it?

Craig: No, I just wanted to stop by and see how my girl was doing tonight. Is that okay?

Sherry: Oh, sure.

Craig: Don't look so excited. It'll go to my head.

Sherry: It's not that I'm not glad to see you. It's just that I was getting ready to go out.

Craig: You can spare a few min-utes away from your girlfriends to be with me, can't you?

Sherry: Yeah, it's just …

Craig: Just what?

Sherry: Just so unexpected. I mean, uh, I just, uh, you know, like to know when you're coming over … so I can look good.

Craig: Sherry, you always look good.

Sherry: Thanks. (*pause*) Well, what do you want to talk about?

Craig: Well, can we sit down?

Sherry: Sure, but like I said, I gotta leave pretty soon.

Craig: All right! I promise I won't take but a few minutes. I just wanted to talk about … us.

Sherry: (*glances over shoulder*) What about us?

Craig: I've just been feeling really good about the other night.

Sherry: Oh, well, I have, too.

Craig: You have?

Sherry: Well, sure. We always have a good time together.

Craig: I'm talking about more than just having a good time together. You know what I mean.

Sherry: Not really.

Craig: (*awkward yet sincere*) Well, you know, the other night when we were talking and you were saying how I was really special to you; you know, different from other guys you've dated and stuff, and I didn't say anything back. Well, I've been thinking. I, uh, you know, like you, too. And I'm sorry I didn't say anything the other night. I guess I wasn't sure, but now I am, and I just wanted to tell you. (*pause*) Didn't know I could talk so much, did you?

Sherry: (*nervous laughter*) No.

Craig: Me neither. So … that's why I came over. What do you think?

Sherry: Well, um, that's really sweet of you, Craig. I like you, too. But why don't we wait and talk about this later when we can have more time together? You know, tomorrow night like we planned. That way we can just talk all night. What do you think?

Craig: Sounds great. I can't wait.

Jack: (*approaches from behind, eating some celery*) Me

Sherry: neither. So will you two hurry it up with this lovey-dovey talk of yours so we can get to the show on time?

Sherry: (*embarrassed and angry*) Jack, go back in the kitchen and I'll be in when we're done!

Jack: Hey, I'm the one you got a date with tonight, remember?

Sherry: I said, go back in the kitch –

Craig: What's going on?

Jack: It's like this, pal …

Sherry: Jack, just shut up!

Jack: Well, excuse me.

Craig: Sherry …

Sherry: Craig, come on, don't act so innocent and naive. You can't tell me that you don't date other girls besides me.

Craig: What if I told you I don't?

Sherry: I wouldn't believe you. I don't know of any guy

that's true blue. So I figure if you can date around, so can I. Right?

Craig: Let me get this straight. All the while you've been seeing me, you've been seeing this guy, too.

Jack: And every other guy.

Sherry: Will you shut up!

Craig: So I'm just one of many.

Sherry: You don't have to say it like that.

Craig: Well, what about all that stuff you said to me, you know, about being different and special?

Sherry: Craig, I don't know what the big deal is.

Craig: Answer me! What about all that you said?

Sherry: Listen, I don't say things I don't mean. You *are* different from other guys and special. But does that mean I have to see you only?

Jack: Yeah, there are others of us

that are just as special.

Sherry: Jack, go to the car.

Jack: Yes, ma'am. (*exits*)

Sherry: Listen, Craig, there's nothing to get upset about. You're seeing other girls and I'm seeing other guys. It's just that now it's out in the open. No big deal. Okay? (**Craig** *just stares at her*) Listen, I gotta get going. Jack's waiting. We'll talk more tomorrow night. Okay? When you leave, just be sure the lights are out and the door's locked. Hey, no harm done, right? (*exits*)

Craig: Right. No harm done.

Song: "Honesty"

Scene II: *Scene is set at a table in a restaurant.* **Craig** *and* **Kelly** *are sitting at the table.* **Waitress** *is taking the order.*

Craig: We'll take two hamburgers, two fries, and – what do you drink?

Kelly: 7-Up.

Craig: One 7-Up and one Pepsi.

Waitress: Is that it?

Craig: Yeah, thanks.

(**Waitress** *exits. From this point on,* **Craig** *is looking around, showing no attention to* **Kelly**.)

Kelly: (*after short silence*) So, how'd you like the movie?

Craig: It was okay.

Kelly: Yeah, I kinda liked it, too. But then I like any movie that's got some horror stuff in it.

Craig: Yeah?

Kelly: Yeah, the bloodier, the better. (*short silence*) So, you got any brothers and sisters?

Craig: Yeah.

Kelly: Well, um, only brothers, only sisters, one of each, older, younger, what?

Craig: (*irritated by the questions*) I've got one of each.

Kelly: Oh. (*pause*) Say, are you always this quiet on dates or is it just me?

Craig: No, I'm usually pretty talkative.

Kelly: Oh, so it's me, then.

Craig: What?

Kelly: Are you looking for someone? I mean, ever since we got here, all you've done is look around.

Craig: What? No, I'm not looking for anyone; just seeing who's here.

Kelly: Well, I'm here.

Craig: Yeah, I know. (*seeing Sherry, Craig suddenly puts his arm around Kelly and begins talking and smiling at her*) Now, what were you saying? So you liked the movie? Boy, I tell you, the gorier the better, right?

Kelly: Huh?

Sherry: (*walks by with Jack and sees Craig*) Hi, Craig.

Craig: (*ignores Sherry*) Yeah, I've got a younger brother and an older sister. My whole family is great. I know you'd love them.

Sherry: Hi, Craig.

Craig: What? Oh, hi, Sherry. How ya doing?

Sherry: (*looks Kelly over*) Pretty good. How about you?

Craig: Couldn't be better. (*squeezes Kelly*) Oh, this is my girlfriend, Kelly.

Sherry: (*unfriendly*) Hi.

Kelly: (*uncomfortable*) Hi.

Craig: So, how are you doing?

Sherry: (*no enthusiasm*) Oh, great. Jack and I are getting married after we graduate.

Craig: Married?! Wow, that's quick.

Sherry: Yeah, well, when it happens, it happens.

Craig: Yeah, right. I know what you mean.

Sherry: Oh, really?

Craig: Yeah, me and Kelly are pretty close. Like I said, I'm doing really good; great, as a matter of fact. I guess it just goes to show you that things usually work out for the best, huh? No harm done?

Sherry: Yeah, I guess so. (**Craig** *begins whispering in* **Kelly's** *ear.*) Well, we've gotta get going. See you around.

Craig: Right. Good luck. (*continues to be attentive to* **Kelly** *until he's sure* **Sherry** *and* **Jack** *are gone. He then removes his arm and returns to his original attitude.*)

Kelly: Why do I have the distinct impression that I have just been used? You mind telling me what that whole thing was all about?

Craig: Nothing. Just be quiet.

Kelly: Just be quiet! Who do you think you are? And what do you think I am that you can just change personality and use me for some kind

of prop in a scene with your old girlfiend?

Craig: Kelly, do me a favor and just shut up.

Kelly: Listen …

Craig: No, you listen. I don't care and I don't need this whining going on in my ear. If you don't like it or me then just leave. On second thought, I'll leave, because I'll tell you something. I don't need you, Sherry, or any other girl or any other person for that matter. I can do just fine on my own. (*exits*)

(*Lights out. Last part of "Honesty."*)

Discussion Questions

1. Have you ever purposely left someone with an impression about you or about your feelings that was not true? Why did you do it?
2. Has someone ever left you with a certain impression about themselves or their feelings – an impression that you later discovered was inaccurate or completely untrue? How did you feel?
3. Have you ever felt used by someone? Or have you deliberately used

another person to accomplish your purposes? Explain.

4. Is it ever right to leave false impressions with people or to use people — even if it's for a "good" reason?